Nazarene
Israel

The Original Faith
of the Apostles

Fully Revised Fourth Edition (v4.01)

By Norman B. Willis

Yeshayahu (Isaiah) 8:20
20 "To the law and to the testimony!
If they do not speak according to this word,
it is because there is no light in them."

Table of Contents:

Tehillim (Psalms) 132:1-5
1 Yahweh, remember David
and all his afflictions;
2 How he swore to Yahweh,
and vowed to the Mighty One of Jacob:
3 "Surely I will not go
into the chamber of my house,
or go up to the comfort of my bed;
4 I will not give sleep to my eyes
or slumber to my eyelids,
5 Until I find a place for Yahweh,
a dwelling place
for the Mighty One of Jacob."

Preface

Readers often ask me what version of Scripture I use. Normally I quote from the New King James Version (NKJV), basically because it is widely trusted and fairly easy to read. However, I also correct the names and terms to the Hebraic forms, for reasons I will explain in this book. When I feel it is helpful to clarify something, or to give additional information, I will place my words in brackets.

Unless noted otherwise, all Hebrew and Aramaic quotes from the Tanach (Old Testament) are from the Hebrew Masoretic Text (MT). Unless noted otherwise, all quotes in Aramaic for the Renewed Covenant (New Testament) are from the Eastern Peshitta. For Greek I will normally quote from the BibleWorks Greek Text (BGT). If I quote anything else, I will try to let you know.

For historical reasons that are too complex to explain here, the Protestant world has come to believe that the apostles first wrote their epistles in Greek. This is not accurate. As we explain in this book, the church fathers tell us the epistles were written in a Semitic tongue (Hebrew or Aramaic, or both). They were translated into Greek afterwards. However, the Hebrew and Aramaic originals are no longer with us, and there is evidence that some of the Greek texts are older than the existing Aramaic texts. For this reason, I normally use the Greek texts for textual analysis.

It is true that all of the texts we have today have been altered over time (including the so-called "original" Hebrew Masoretic Text). It is important to know this because anti-missionaries will oftentimes point to some of the discrepancies between the Hebrew Masoretic Text and the Renewed Covenant texts, and then suggest that the Renewed Covenant is wrong, because it does agree with the Masoretic text. Without getting into too much detail here, the Hebrew Masoretic Text dates back only to 900-1100 CE, and it is the result of an Orthodox Jewish attempt to "fix" (or standardize) the texts in keeping with Orthodox Jewish traditions (one of which is to reject the deity of Yeshua [Jesus]). This is not cause for despair. We simply have to realize that our Orthodox brethren made some small changes and alterations to the Text over the course of centuries, and then realize that Yahweh is faithful to give us what we need, when we need it—and that by careful scholarship we can deduce what has been changed and why.

I have chosen to use the Hebraic names and terms for reasons I hope will be clear by the time you finish reading this study. In many places, Yahweh (Jehovah) tells us that He is zealous for His name, and He promises to reward those who know His name.

> Tehillim (Psalms) 91:14
> 14 "Because he has set his love upon Me, therefore I will deliver him; I will set him on high, because he has known My name."

If it is clear that Yahweh says we should know and use His name, the exact pronunciation of His name is a subject of some discussion. I pronounce His name as Yahweh (or Yahuweh), and I will write *Yahweh* in this book. If you feel convicted of another pronunciation, (Yehovah, etc.), please substitute it as you read.

In Hebrew, the term for *God* is *Elohim*. I will use the Hebraic term in this book because the word *God* is actually the name of a Germanic sun deity, and we are told not to use the names of other deities (e.g., Exodus 23:13). Further, I will normally use the name *Yeshua* for the name of our Messiah, as that is what His mother called him, and I feel it is more respectful to call Him by His actual name. (For a more complete discussion of the divine names, please see "The Set apart Names," in *Nazarene Scripture Studies, Volume 1*.)

Because this book is a primer, and because many people will read individual chapters on the Internet, I ask for your patience as I give the English names the first time they are used in each chapter. I will then use the Hebraic names for the rest of the chapter.

I know that nothing done of man is perfect, but I hope that this book will help advance an understanding of the faith our Messiah originally taught His apostles to keep.

If you have questions or constructive suggestions, please write me: servants@nazareneisrael.org.

Norman B. Willis
In the Ephraimite Dispersion,
Estimated 6014 (2014 CE).

Introduction: My Testimony

In 1999, the Creator saved me by a miracle that was so powerful, I knew instantly that I would be giving the rest of my life to Him. Serving Him has often been difficult, but it was the best choice I ever made. I have never regretted it.

Because of the nature of the miracle, it was clear that it could only have been the Creator Yahweh (Jehovah) who had saved me—but what I did not know was whether or not the Messiah had already come. If I was to serve our heavenly Father the right way, the first thing I had to do was to show myself, from the Tanach (Old Testament) alone, whether or not the Messiah had already come.

Once I could see in the Tanach that the Messiah had already come once, the next thing I needed to know was which version of the faith He had come to teach, because Scripture tells us to contend earnestly for the faith that was delivered to the saints.

> Yehudah (Jude) 3
> 3 Beloved, while I was very diligent to write to you concerning our common salvation, I found it necessary to write to you exhorting you to contend earnestly for the faith which was once for all delivered to the saints.

I did not want to assume that the faith I was taught as a child was the correct one. There were many different denominations, but at most only one of them could be correct. I needed to know which of them, if any, was the faith the Messiah had originally taught.

I went back to the church I was raised in, but I did not stay. The pastor openly contradicted the Messiah in his sermons, using one verse to explain away another. He said, "The Bible says it is better to give than to receive, but that is wrong. Any child knows it is better to receive than to give—and doesn't the Bible say we are to be like little children?" I knew I could not stay there.

I left my old church and went to an Episcopal cathedral with a powerful preacher. I loved his sermons, and my love for Yahweh grew. After taking communion, I felt the Spirit fall on me, as if someone had hooked me up to some unseen electric source. I began seeing the world through new eyes, and hearing things with new ears. It was as if the world was transformed before me.

When the preacher retired a few months later, the steering committee hired a gay pastor to take his place. He was funny, and he made us all laugh, but in his introductory sermon he told jokes about how much he hated the parable of the wedding feast. He told the congregation to disregard it, as he said it did not apply to us today. Then, at the end of his sermon he said he wanted to raise millions of dollars so they could finish remodeling the cathedral. It seemed that a beautiful building was more important to him than obeying the Messiah's words. When I asked Yahweh about it, I opened my Scriptures, and there was 2 Timothy 4:3-4.

TimaTheus Bet (2 Timothy) 4:3-4
3 For the time will come when they will not endure sound doctrine, but according to their own desires, because they have itching ears, they will heap up for themselves teachers;
4 and they will turn their ears away from the truth, and be turned aside to fables.

That was exactly what I saw. The congregants seemed relieved when the pastor told them the Scriptures did not apply to them. It made them happy. Evidently they wanted someone to tell them that as long as they went through the motions and made a good show, they did not have to take the Messiah's words to heart, or live by them. But that wasn't *church* to me.

Where were the real believers? Scripture said that fellowship was important, so I had to find others who wanted to serve their Messiah and King. Not knowing what else to do, or where else to go, I thought perhaps I could find real faith among the remnants of the old pioneer communities in rural America. I would have to leave the cities, but I did not care what it cost—I had to find other believers who wanted to live for Him.

> Mattityahu (Matthew) 13:45-46
> 45 "Again, the kingdom of heaven is like a merchant seeking beautiful pearls,
> 46 who, when he had found one pearl of great price, went and sold all that he had and bought it."

I moved to an area in eastern Washington that I knew from my childhood. It was a place where roadside fruit stands were left unattended. People picked out the fruit they wanted, weighed their purchases, made change in the money box, and everything was done on the honor system. If faith was to be found anywhere in America, I felt surely I could find it there in the heartland where the Bible was still part of everyday life.

Praying for direction, I moved to a small rural town that was to be my new home. The Seventh-day Adventists left a flyer in my mailbox that asked, "When was the Sabbath changed to Sunday? And where do the prophecies say that the day of weekly worship would ever be changed?" I could not answer that, so I went to study with them. The Sabbath seemed to be the right day, but they kept other holidays that the Bible did not say to keep, such as Christmas and Easter. After doing some research, I realized the Bible never said any of the days of worship should be changed. It also said not to keep Asherah or Ishtar, which were just different forms of the name Easter.

Melachim Aleph (1 Kings) 18:19
19 "Now therefore, send and gather all Israel to me on Mount Carmel, the four hundred and fifty prophets of Baal, and the four hundred prophets of Asherah [Easter], who eat at Jezebel's table."

Thinking they would want to know, I tried sharing this information with the people at church. They humored me for a while, but eventually the church elders took me aside and implied that if I wanted to stay there, I needed to stop asking so many questions. I was baffled. How could they see that the Sabbath had never changed, but miss the fact that Christmas and Easter were not commanded? It was as if they were still partially blinded.

My neighbors, it turned out, were Messianic Jews— Jews who believe Yeshua (Jesus) is the Messiah. They kept the Old Testament, as well as the New. Instead of Sunday, Christmas, and Easter, they only kept the days that Scripture said to keep. When I asked them about their beliefs, they replied, "If Yahweh does not tell us to do it, then why should we do it? How does that honor Him?" I could not answer that question, so I began to study with them. We met in their house on the Sabbath and throughout the week to talk about His word.

As Yahweh began awakening me to the truth, I became angry at the church for teaching principles that are not supported by His word, or actually contradict His word. Some of my earlier writings reflected this anger and frustration, but Yahweh showed me how the lies of the church were always prophesied.

> Yirmeyahu (Jeremiah) 16:19
> 19 Yahweh, my strength and my fortress,
> My refuge in the day of affliction.
> The gentiles shall come to You
> From the ends of the earth and say,
> "Surely our fathers have inherited lies,
> Worthlessness and unprofitable things."

Over time, and by word of mouth, I met other believers and seekers, both in person and on the Internet. Many of them had the same types of questions. As I studied things out, I wrote my studies down, and sent them out to my friends on the Internet—and then they began forwarding them to their friends. Soon I put up a website and posted all of my past studies. As we learned more, sometimes I would have to re-write the studies and send out corrected versions. I was happy to do it because it did not matter whether or not *I* was right—only the studies needed to be right.

As we kept studying, the studies got longer, and more complex. As we saw how the various studies tied in with each other, eventually it became clear that we needed to put everything together in one book, to give the reader a better sense of perspective. Although we have rewritten and updated it many times, this is the book you are reading now—our discoveries about what the Hebrew Scriptures truly say.

I invite you to come along with me as I share some of the things I've learned. I don't want you to believe anything just because I say it—I only want you to use this book as a study guide. I pray that you will be like the noble Bereans who studied the Scriptures daily to see if the things they were being taught were correct.

Ma'asei (Acts) 17:10-12
10 Then the brethren immediately sent Paul and Silas away by night to Berea. When they arrived, they went into the synagogue of the Jews.
11 These were more noble-minded than those in Thessalonica, in that they received the word with all readiness, and searched the Scriptures daily to find out whether these things were so.
12 Therefore many of them believed; and also not a few of the Greeks, prominent women as well as men.

What Was the Original Faith?

When I was a child, I was taught in church that the words *Christian* and *Nazarene* were synonyms, and that they referred to the same group of people. Years later, I realized that this was not correct. One of the Catholic Church founders, Epiphanius of Salamis, wrote a book in the early fourth century called *Panarion* (*Against Heresies*), in which he condemned a group called the *Nazarenes* for practicing *Jewish* Christianity. That is, the Nazarenes believed on the Messiah, yet they still kept the original Jewish rites of circumcision, the Sabbath, and the laws of Moshe (Moses).

> "The Nazarenes do not differ in any essential thing from them [the Orthodox Jews], since they practice the customs and doctrines prescribed by Jewish Law; except that they believe in Christ. They believe in the resurrection of the dead, and that the universe was created by God. They preach that God is One, and that Jesus Christ is His Son. They are very learned in the Hebrew language. They read the Law [the Law of Moshe].… Therefore they differ…from the true Christians because they fulfill until now [such] Jewish rites as the circumcision, Sabbath and others."
> [Epiphanius of Salamis, "Against Heresies," Panarion 29, 7, pp. 41, 402]

Since Epiphanius was Catholic, his condemnation of the Nazarenes meant that the Catholic Christians and the Nazarenes could not possibly have been the same group of people—but they were two separate groups.

Yet if the Messiah and His apostles were Jewish, why did Epiphanius condemn the Nazarenes for practicing *Jewish* Christianity? To answer that question, let us look at the works of Marcel Simon, a late Catholic expert on the first century. Even though Marcel Simon was a devout Catholic, he disagreed with Epiphanius, saying that Epiphanius knew that the Catholic Church did not descend from the apostles.

> "They [Nazarenes] are characterized essentially by their tenacious attachment to Jewish observances. If they became heretics in the eyes of the Mother Church, it is simply because they remained fixed on outmoded positions. They well represent, [even] though Epiphanius is energetically refusing to admit it, the very direct descendants of that primitive community, of which our author [Epiphanius] knows that it was designated by the Jews, by the same name, of 'Nazarenes'."
> [First Century expert Marcel Simon, Judéo-christianisme, pp. 47-48.]

Marcel Simon tells us Epiphanius knew it was the Nazarenes who descended from James, John, Peter, Paul, Andrew, and the rest; yet both Epiphanius and Marcel Simon called the Nazarenes "heretics" because they continued to keep the same faith the Messiah had taught them. But isn't that what Scripture says to do?

> Yehudah (Jude) 3
> 3 Beloved, while I was very diligent to write to you concerning our common salvation, I found it necessary to write to you, exhorting you to contend earnestly for the faith which was once for all delivered to the saints.

18

If Jude tells us to "contend earnestly" for the faith which was "once for all" delivered to the saints, then isn't that the faith we should keep?

As I began reading more about the Catholic Church, I began to see that there were many in the Catholic Church who felt that somehow they had the authority to change what the Scriptures taught.

> "Some theologians have held that God likewise directly determined the Sunday as the day of worship in the New Law, [and] that He Himself has explicitly substituted the Sunday for the Sabbath. But this theory is now entirely abandoned. It is now commonly held that God simply gave His Church the power to set aside whatever day or days she would deem suitable as Holy Days. The Church chose Sunday, the first day of the week, and in the course of time added other days as holy days."
> [John Laux, A Course in Religion for Catholic High Schools and Academies (1936), vol. 1, P. 51.]

Was John Laux saying that the Church had the authority to change the Father's word? What sense did that make? It didn't make any sense, but other Catholics asserted the same thing.

> "But you may read the Bible from Genesis to Revelation, and you will not find a single line authorizing the sanctification of Sunday. The Scriptures enforce the religious observance of Saturday, a day which we [the Church] never sanctify."
> [James Cardinal Gibbons, The Faith of our Fathers, 88th ed., pp. 89.]

19

Many high ranking Catholic Church authorities admit that the Catholic Church had changed the days of worship on her own.

"Question: Have you any other way of proving that the Church has power to institute festivals of precept?
"Answer: Had she not such power, she could not have done that in which all modern religionists agree with her-she could not have substituted the observance of Sunday, the first day of the week, for the observance of Saturday, the seventh day, a change for which there is no Scriptural authority."
[Stephen Keenan, A Doctrinal Catechism 3rd ed., p. 174.]

Thus the Catholic Church claims it had the power to change the days of worship simply because they did it (and got away with it)? That doesn't match up with Scripture at all! Instead, we are told not to add or take away from His word.

Devarim (Deuteronomy) 12:32
32 "Whatever I command you, be careful to observe it; you shall not add to it nor take away from it."

The Creator had told Israel to keep the seventh-day Sabbath (Saturday) as His official day of rest, and it was never prophesied that it would change.

Shemote (Exodus) 20:8
8 "Remember the Sabbath day, to keep it set apart (holy)."

What happened? Had the Catholics suppressed the original Nazarene Israelite faith? And if so, then how can we rebuild the original faith for those who want to practice it?

And can we verify all of this from Scripture? Do the Scriptures tell us there were two separate groups of people in the first century, the Christians and the Nazarenes? And if so, then which group do the Scriptures say the apostles belonged to?

Yeshua the Nazarene Israelite

In the last chapter we saw that by the fourth century the Christians and the Nazarenes were two completely separate faiths—and that the Christians persecuted the Nazarenes. History indicates that the Messiah Yeshua was a Nazarene. However, history is not enough—we need to prove everything from Scripture. So, was Yeshua a *Christian*, or was He a *Nazarene*?

The Renewed Covenant (New Testament) tells us the Messiah Yeshua would be called a Nazarene because He grew up in a town called Nazareth (Natseret, נצרת). Let us look at the Aramaic Peshitta.

Matthew 2:23 MGI	Eastern Peshitta
23 And he came [and] lived in the city that is called Nazareth, [so] that it would be fulfilled what was spoken by the prophet: "He shall be called a Nazarene."	ואתא עמר במדינתא דמתקריא נצרת איך דנתמלא מדם דאתאמר בנביא דנצריא נתקרא

Sometimes people look for this reference in English translations of the Tanach (Old Testament), but they don't find it because the reference is to the Hebrew of Isaiah 11:1, where it was said that a Rod (King David) would grow from the stem of Jesse, David's father—and that a Branch (Yeshua) would grow up out of his roots. The Hebrew word for "branch" is *Netzer* (נצר) (shown in the shaded area).

Isaiah 11:1 NKJV 11 There shall come forth a Rod from the stem of Jesse, and a Branch [Netzer] shall grow out of His roots.	Hebrew Masoretic Text וְיָצָא חֹטֶר מִגֵּזַע (1) יִשָׁי׀ וְנֵצֶר מִשָּׁרָשָׁיו יִפְרֶה

Matthew is shown in Aramaic and Isaiah is in Hebrew, yet by omitting the vowels we can see that Nazarene (נצריא) and Netzer (נצר) have the same root (נצר), therefore it was correct for Matthew to say that Yeshua would be called a Nazarene.

In Hebrew and Aramaic thought, if Yeshua was called a Nazarene, then His followers would also be Nazarenes. This is why, in Acts 24:5, the Pharisees accused the Apostle Shaul (Paul) not of being a Christian, but of being a ringleader of the sect of the Nazarenes.

Ma'asei (Acts) 24:5
5 "For we have found this man a plague, a creator of dissension among all the Jews throughout the world, and a ringleader of the sect [KJV: heresy] of the Nazarenes."

But why did the Pharisees say the Apostle Shaul was part of a sect? In Hebrew, the term for "sect" is *min* (מן), which means, a *departure*. The idea is that the faith Yahweh gave Israel at Mount Sinai is the one true and correct faith—and that everything else *departs* from that truth. So for the Pharisees to say Shaul was part of a "sect" was to say he had departed from the truth. Shaul, however, felt he had not left the truth, because he still believed everything that was written in the Torah and in the Prophets.

Ma'asei (Acts) 24:14
14 "But this I confess to you, that according to the Way which they call a sect [KJV: heresy], so I worship the Elohim [God] of my fathers, believing all things which are written in the Law [of Moshe] and in the Prophets."

We will revisit this topic in later chapters, once we have some more background information. However, for right now, let us note that Shaul never claimed he was a Christian. Rather, he claimed to be an Israelite—and he said he still believed all things that are written in the Law and in the Prophets. This is something most Christians cannot honestly say.

While the word "sect" can refer to a cult, mostly it refers to a sub-section of something larger. For example, Christendom can be divided into different sub-sects (Catholic, Protestant, and Orthodox, for example)—and inside these sects there are still more sub-sects. For example, inside Protestantism there are Lutherans, Baptists, Methodists, Pentecostals, etc. Ironically, the members of some sects consider the members of all other sects to be heretics—and this attitude is Scriptural, even if it is wrongly applied.

Judaism is similarly exclusory, and fragmented. The Orthodox Jews form the largest sect, but there are also Conservative Jews, Reform Jews, Karaite Jews, Hasidic Jews, and others. The Orthodox Jews consider all of the other sects to be heretics (just as they called Shaul a heretic in Acts 24:5, above).

It helps to understand that Scripture names groups of people according to their attitudes and beliefs. That is, it labels them according to their spirits. This is why the same sects still exist today as existed in the first century, just with different names, because the same spirits are still around today.

First Century	Today
Pharisees	Orthodox
Hellenists/Greek Jews	Reform
Nazarenes	Nazarenes
"Pharisees who believed"	Messianic Jews

The sect of the Pharisees of the first century changed their name in the Middle Ages, and now they are called the Orthodox Jews. The Karaite Jews of today descend from the sect of the Sadducees. Even though there is no direct connection, the Hellenists of the first century (also called the "Greek" Jews in some translations) are similar to the Reform Jews of today, because they have the same kind of spirit. As we will see later, the rabbinic Messianic Jews of today are like the "Pharisees who believed" of Acts 15. (We will talk about the Messianic Jews in more detail as we go along.) Because it will help us later on, we will spend a bit more time learning who these groups are now.

Scripture names people according to their beliefs, and their walk. For example, Israel is called Israel because they believe on Israel's Elohim. However, when we read about the Greeks (Hellenists) of the Renewed Covenant, these are not ethnic Greeks, but less devout Jews who obeyed an invader, rather than Yahweh. About two hundred years before Yeshua, the Hellenic King Antiochus invaded Judea, and he commanded all of the Israelites to forget Yahweh, and to worship Greek gods instead. Those who obeyed him (even partially) were called "Greeks" (or Hellenists) as a derogatory term, because they had adopted Greek customs and traditions.

Maqabim Aleph (1 Maccabees) 1:41-43
41 Moreover King Antiochus wrote his whole kingdom, that all should be one people,
42 And every one should leave his laws: so all the heathen agreed according to the commandment of the king.
43 Yea, many also of the Israelites consented to his religion, and sacrificed unto idols, and profaned the Sabbath.

It was common to name people according to their faith until the Enlightenment (i.e., the Luciferism) of the seventeenth and eighteenth centuries. This is also when Reform Judaism arose. Reform Jews feel it is okay to blend faiths, and they are open to hearing about other faiths. This is the same spirit as the Greeks (Hellenists) of the first century—and this may be why the Pharisees asked themselves if Yeshua was going to go teach among the Greeks outside the land.

Yochanan (John) 7:34-35
34 "You will seek Me and not find Me, and where I am you cannot come."
35 Then the Jews said among themselves, "Where does He intend to go that we shall not find Him? Does He intend to go to the Dispersion among the Greeks and teach the Greeks?"

Later we will see that Christianity probably did arise among the Hellenic Jews, but what we need to see here is that Scripture does not label us according to our genetics, because Yahweh does not care about our genetics, but our hearts. This is also why Yochanan HaMatbil (John the Baptist) told the Pharisees and the Sadducees that their genetics was no guarantee of salvation.

Mattityahu (Matthew) 3:7-9

7 But when he saw many of the Pharisees and Sadducees coming to his immersion [baptism], he said to them, "Brood of vipers! Who warned you to flee from the wrath to come?

8 Therefore bear fruits worthy of repentance,

9 and do not think to say to yourselves, 'We have Avraham as our father.' For I say to you that Elohim is able to raise up children to Avraham from these stones!"

Today (after the Enlightenment) there is thought to be a difference between being an Israeli and being an Israelite. To be an Israeli (i.e., to live in the land of Israel) you need paperwork from the state. However, to be an Israelite, you simply convert to the worship of the Elohim of Israel, as Root (Ruth) did.

Root (Ruth) 1:16-17

16 But Ruth said: "Entreat me not to leave you, Or to turn back from following after you; For wherever you go, I will go; And wherever you lodge, I will lodge; Your people shall be my people, and your Elohim, my Elohim.

17 Where you die, I will die, And there will I be buried. Yahweh do so to me, and more also, If anything but death parts you and me."

Ironically, while Ruth became an Israelite the instant she pledged allegiance to the Elohim of Israel, if she came to the border of Israel today without paperwork from the government, she would likely be turned away. This kind of distinction does not exist in Scripture, for in Scripture, however you worship (and however you self-identify), that is who you are (and that is what you are called).

Bearing all of this in mind, let us note, then, that the Apostle Shaul self-identified as an Israelite (a follower of the Elohim of Israel), and not as a Christian.

> Qorintim Bet (2 Corinthians) 11:22
> 22 Are they Hebrews? So am I. Are they Israelites? So am I. Are they the seed of Abraham? So am I.

Shaul told the Jews in Rome that Elohim had not cast away His people Israel, for he also was an Israelite.

> Romim (Romans) 11:1
> 1 I say then, has Elohim cast away His people? Certainly not! For I also am an Israelite, of the seed of Abraham, of the tribe of Benjamin.

Then, when Shaul was taken to Rome, the Jews there wanted to hear about the Nazarene sect of the Israelite faith (rather than about torahless Christianity).

> Ma'asei (Acts) 28:22
> 22 "But we desire to hear from you what you think; for concerning this sect, we know that it is spoken against everywhere."

The difference between the original Nazarene faith and torahless Christianity has a lot to do with what might be called zealousness for the three Ls:

1. The land of Israel
2. The Hebrew language
3. The law of Moshe

The Nazarenes clung zealously to their inheritance in the land of Israel, the Hebrew language, and the law of

Moshe, because as we will see in the next chapter, they understood the law of Moshe to be a marital covenant between them and Yahweh Elohim, which they had to obey if they wanted to be part of the bride.

In contrast, the Christian church teaches that the law is not a marital covenant, and that it has been done away with ("and good riddance!" many of them would say).

The Torah: a Marital Covenant

Although the term *Christian* is not used until Acts 11, the first torahless Christian probably appears as early as Mark 9:38. There, Yochanan (John) alerts Yeshua of a man who was casting out demons in His name, yet who was not *following* the disciples.

Marqaus (Mark) 9:38-39
38 Now Yochanan (John) answered Him, saying, "Teacher, we saw someone who does not follow us casting out demons in Your name, and we forbade him because he does not follow us."
39 But Yeshua said, "Do not forbid him, for no one who works a miracle in My name can soon afterward speak evil of Me."

Why was this man probably the first Christian? The answer lies in understanding what it means to *follow* the Messiah. Christianity teaches that so long as we believe on the Messiah, and call upon His name, we are *following* Him. In other words, the Christians teach that so long as one *thinks* Yeshua is the Messiah, they do not need to walk as He walked, or keep the law of Moshe (Moses). (And in fact, most Christians believe the Messiah came to do away with the law of Moshe.)

Mark 9:38 shows us the Christian doctrine is logically impossible. If all one must do to *follow* Yeshua is to call upon His name, then how could Yochanan say there was a man who was even casting out demons in Yeshua's name, who was not *following* Him? Clearly, anyone who casts out a demon in Yeshua's name is calling upon His name (and believes on Him)—and yet Yochanan said that this man was not *following*.

The reason the Christian church misses the mark is that it uses the wrong definition of the word *belief*. The church uses the Hellenic (Greek) definition which is based on thoughts rather than actions. In Hellenic thought, *thinking* and *believing* can be synonyms—and that is why the Christian church teaches that if we *think* Yeshua is the Messiah, then we *believe* He is the Messiah—and that this thought is enough to save us.

The problem with this Hellenic model is that it does not call for obedience to any external standard (such as the law of Moshe). As long as you *think* Yeshua is the Messiah, you think you can rest on whichever day of the week you want (and you can do as you see fit). The Hellenic model says there is nothing to obey.

In contrast, the Hebrew language is based on function and action. Because the Hellenic model leads to a wrong result, the Nazarenes reject the Hellenic model as being flawed.

In Hebraic thought, man was created to purify himself by obeying Elohim's will (as codified in the law of Moshe). Therefore, a Hebrew assumes that if we truly *believe* on Him, then we will want to follow His laws— and conversely, if we do not follow His laws, there is no proof that we believe on Him (and, therefore, by logical extension, we do not truly believe).

The Hebrew word for *law* is *Torah*. This word is often translated as *law* because the wishes of the King of the universe carry the weight of law. However, the word *Torah* actually translates as *instructions*. In context it refers to the *instructions* given to Yahweh's bride Israel fifty days after she left Egypt. It was given to her as a wedding covenant, to which she said, "I do."

Shemote (Exodus) 19:8
8 Then all the people answered together and said, "All that Yahweh has spoken, we will do."

The idea was that if Israel would follow Yahweh's Torah, and purify herself according to it, she would become more pleasing to Him. That way, Yahweh would want to take her as a bride unto Him forever. The children of Israel agreed to these conditions when they said, "I do," at the foot of Mount Sinai. In light of this knowledge, we can see why it is problematic that the Christians would say it is not necessary to keep the Torah, especially when Moshe tells us Yahweh gave the Torah to Israel for her own good.

Devarim (Deuteronomy) 10:12-13
12 "And now, Israel, what has Yahweh your Elohim asked of you, except to fear Yahweh your Elohim, to walk in all His ways, and to love Him; and to serve Yahweh your Elohim with all your heart, and with all your soul;
13 to keep the commandments of Yahweh, and His statutes, which I am commanding you today for your good."

Christianity believes the Bridegroom came to set the bride free from something that was given to her for her own good—but what sense does that make?

If we realize that the King of the universe gave us His bridal instructions so we could become a more pleasing bride for Him, then we can understand passages such as 1 John 2:3-5, which tell us that unless we truly desire to keep the Bridegroom's commandments, we do not really know (or love) the Bridegroom.

Yochanan Aleph (1 John) 2:3-5
3 And by this we know that we know Him; if we keep His commandments.
4 He who says, "I have known Him," but [who is] not keeping His Commandments is a liar; and the Truth is not in that one.
5 But whoever keeps His word, truly in this one the love of Elohim has been perfected: By this we know we are in Him.

We are also told that torahlessness is sin.

Yochanan Aleph (1 John) 3:4
4 Whoever commits sin also commits torahlessness; for sin is torahlessness.

If sin is torahlessness, torahlessness is sin. Therefore, if we disobey His bridal covenant, we are sinning, and He has no reason to wed us.

Some Christians will cite John 3:16 to say that there is no need to keep the marital covenant, because so long as we believe on Yeshua, we have eternal life.

Yochanan (John) 3:16
16 For Elohim so loved the world that He gave His only begotten Son; that whosoever believeth in Him should not perish, but have everlasting life.

John 3:16 is plainly true, but we already saw that the Christians define the word "believe" incorrectly. Notice that twenty verses later, John the Baptist tells us that unless we *obey* the Son (who wants us to keep His marital covenant), the wrath of Elohim will remain upon us (and we will not be taken in marriage). We will quote here from the New American Standard Updated (NASU).

34

John 3:36 NASU
36 "He who believes in the Son has eternal life;
but he who does not obey the Son will not see
life, but the wrath of God abides on him."

The King James translators, however, did not realize
that the Torah is the bridal covenant—so perhaps with
the best of intentions they mistranslated John 3:36.

John 3:36, KJV	BGT John 3:36 ὁ πιστεύων
36 "He that believeth on the Son hath everlasting life: and he that believeth not the Son shall not see life; but the wrath of God abideth on him."	εἰς τὸν υἱὸν ἔχει ζωὴν αἰώνιον· ὁ δὲ ἀπειθῶν τῷ υἱῷ οὐκ ὄψεται ζωήν, ἀλλ᾽ ἡ ὀργὴ τοῦ θεοῦ μένει ἐπ᾽ αὐτόν.

The phrase "believeth not" is incorrectly translated. It is
Strong's G#544, apeithoon (ἀπειθῶν), which means to
disbelieve, but in the sense of willful and perverse
disobedience.

NT:544 apeitheo (ap-i-theh'-o); from NT:545; to
disbelieve (wilfully and perversely):
KJV - not believe, disobedient, obey not,
unbelieving.

The NASU rendering is therefore more accurate:

John 3:36 NASU
36 "He who believes in the Son has eternal life;
but he who does not obey the Son will not see
life, but the wrath of God abides on him."

If the marital covenant has been done away with (as Christianity suggests), then there should be nothing to disobey—but clearly there is, or John would not warn us against willful and perverse disobedience. Further, if we look up the reference to NT:545 (above), we see that we are warned against being disobedient in an unpersuadable way, or being obstinate. This might seem like an apt description of Christian insistence that the law is done away with.

> NT:545 apeithes (ap-i-thace'); from NT:1 (as a negative particle) and NT:3982; unpersuadable, i.e. contumacious:
> KJV - disobedient.

Why do Christian apologists teach that the Torah is an impossible, unnecessary burden that is too difficult to keep? Do they not realize that they contradict what the Apostle John said in his first epistle?

> Yochanan Aleph (1 John) 5:2-3
> 2 By this we know that we love the children of Elohim: when we love Elohim, and keep His commandments.
> 3 For this is the love of Elohim: that we keep His commandments, and His commandments are not burdensome.

When we love Yeshua, it is not a burden to do what he asks—it is a joy. Further, if the Son of the living Elohim wants us to prepare ourselves to become His bride, is it not a burden, but a thrill!

The Nazarenes do not find Yeshua's commandments burdensome, because they love their Husband, and want to please Him in any way they can. So why do the Christians rejoice at the thought of being set free from

His marital covenant? (And which one of these two philosophies seems more motivated by love for the Bridegroom?)

The church teaches that the Messiah came to nail the Torah to the cross (and therefore, there are no more commandments to obey). They also teach that the desire to obey Elohim's commandments is legalism, and should be strictly avoided. But why do they teach this? Do they not realize they are directly contradicting Yeshua, who told us in the plainest of terms *not* to think He had come to destroy the Torah (but only to fulfill a part of the prophecies)?

> Mattityahu (Matthew) 5:17-19
> 17 "Do not think that I came to destroy the Torah or the Prophets. I did not come to destroy but to fulfill.
> 18 For assuredly, I say to you, till heaven and earth pass away, one jot or one tittle will by no means pass from the Torah till all is fulfilled.
> 19 Whoever therefore breaks one of the least of these commandments, and teaches men so, shall be called least in the kingdom of heaven; but whoever does and teaches them, he shall be called great in the kingdom of heaven."

There are many prophecies in the Torah and in the Prophets, and Yeshua came to fulfill some of them— yet others still need to be fulfilled. Yeshua said *not* to think that He came to do away with them. In fact, He clearly warns us that whoever breaks one of the least of the commandments, and teaches men so, shall be called least in the kingdom of heaven.

Ironically, when confronted with Yeshua's words, many Christians will search through Shaul's (Paul's) letters, looking for something they can use to explain Yeshua's words away. When asked why they do this, they don't have a good answer.

Some Christians say Shaul's words explain how we should interpret Yeshua's words. However, this is not good scholarship. The Apostle Peter (Kepha) warned us that Shaul's writings were difficult to understand—and that even in his day there was a group of "untaught and unstable" believers who twisted Shaul's words in order to justify a torahless agenda.

> Kepha Bet (2 Peter) 3:15-17
> 15 And think of the long-suffering of our Master as salvation [literally: Yeshua], as also our beloved brother Shaul wrote to you, according to the wisdom given to him;
> 16 As also in all his epistles, speaking in them concerning these things, in which some things are hard to understand, which the untaught and unstable twist, to their destruction, as also the rest of the Scriptures.
> 17 Then beloved, you being fore-warned, watch; lest being led by the error of torahlessness you should fall from your own steadfastness.

Let's think about this—who was it in the first century who believed on Yeshua, but who also twisted Shaul's words to suggest that the Torah and the Prophets were done away with? Could it be the same group of people who today believe on "Jesus," and tell us that the words of "Paul" tell us that the Torah and the Prophets have been done away with?

Is it possible that the very people Kepha wrote to forewarn us about were the Christians? Yes, that is exactly the case—and to understand how we can protect ourselves from being led astray by the error of torahlessness, let us learn more about the Apostle Shaul's epistles, and what the animal sacrifices were really all about.

About Animal Sacrifices for Sin

In Matthew 22, Yeshua quotes two verses from the Torah to show that love has always been at the heart of the Torah.

Mattityahu (Matthew) 22:37-40
37 Yeshua said to him, "'You shall love Yahweh your Elohim with all your heart, with all your soul, and with all your mind.' [Deuteronomy 6:5]
38 This is the first and great commandment.
39 And the second is like it: 'You shall love your neighbor as yourself.' [Leviticus 19:18]
40 On these two commandments hang all the Torah and the Prophets."

Christian apologists twist this passage to make it sound like love renders the marital covenant null and void, since the marital covenant always depended on love. However, that makes no sense. If a marriage depends on love, how does love do away with the marriage? (And if you love your spouse, does that mean your marriage is now done away with?)

The church tells us that the Torah is too difficult for any human being to keep, even though Moshe (Moses) tells us the opposite. Moshe tells us that the word is very near to us, that we may do it.

Deuteronomy (Devarim) 30:11-14
11 "For this commandment which I command you today is not too mysterious for you; nor is it far off.
12 It is not in heaven, that you should say, 'Who will ascend into heaven for us and bring it to us, that we may hear it and do it?'

13 Nor is it beyond the sea, that you should say, 'Who will go over the sea for us and bring it to us, that we may hear it and do it?'
14 But the word is very near you, in your mouth and in your heart, that you may do it."

Christian scholars tell us it was always impossible for Israel to keep the Torah. However, that would make Yahweh out to be a cruel torturer. It would mean He freed the children of Israel from physical bondage in Egypt, only to put them into spiritual bondage in the Torah, requiring something that could never be done so He could reject them cruelly in the end. But does that sound like our loving heavenly Father?

True, Shaul (Paul) did tell the Galatians that the Torah can be a kind of a curse if they mistakenly believe they can earn their salvation by works of the law.

> Galatim (Galatians) 3:10-14
> 10 For as many as are of the works of the Law are under the curse; for it is written, "Cursed is everyone who does not continue in all things which are written in the book of the Torah, to do them."
> 11 But that no one is justified by the Torah in the sight of Elohim is evident, for "the just shall live by faith."
> 12 Yet the Torah is not of faith, but "the man who does them shall live by them."
> 13 Messiah has redeemed us from the curse of the Torah, having become a curse for us (for it is written, "Cursed is everyone who hangs on a tree"),
> 14 that the blessing of Avraham might come upon the Gentiles in Messiah Yeshua, that we might receive the promise of the Spirit through faith.

The key to understanding Shaul is to remember that he always labeled people according to how they believed they got saved. When he talks about those who are *of* the works of the law, he is not talking about Nazarene Israelites who *obey* the law. Rather, he is talking about those who believe they receive salvation *as a direct result* of having performed the works of the law as a kind of a "checklist" for salvation. (This is a fairly apt description of our Pharisee/Orthodox brothers.)

Shaul says that if you believe you are saved as a result of doing works with your hands, then you really are under a curse, because you feel compelled to continue doing the works of your hands in the vain hope that this will somehow save you. However, no one is saved as a result of doing things with his hands, for the just shall be saved (and hence, live) by faith. Yet even though the specific points of law in the Torah are not *of faith*, those who do them (such as the Nazarene Israelites) shall live by them.

If we are willing to receive it, Messiah took the curse (of believing we can save ourselves by doing things with our own hands) upon Himself, having become accursed for us (so to speak), that we might receive the promise that was given to Avraham because of his faith. Yet Shaul cannot mean we should not obey what is written in the Torah, because we will see that he himself obeyed all that was written in the Torah.

Many Christians are astonished to learn that the apostles still performed the animal sacrifices, even many years after Yeshua's resurrection. To see this, let us start in Acts 18:18, where the Apostle Shaul had shaved his head, for he had taken a vow.

Ma'asei (Acts) 18:18
18 So Shaul still remained a good while. Then he took leave of the brethren and sailed for Syria, and Priscilla and Aquila were with him. He shaved his head at Cenchrea, for he had taken a vow.

The only vow in Scripture which calls for shaving one's head is the Nazirite vow, found in Numbers 6. When one separates (ends) a Nazirite vow, one shaves one's head, and then goes up to the temple, where one offers three animal sacrifices, one of which is a sacrifice for sin (verse 14).

Bemidbar (Numbers) 6:13-18
13 Now this is the Torah of the Nazirite: When the days of his separation are fulfilled, he shall be brought to the door of the tabernacle of meeting.
14 And he shall present his offering to Yahweh: one male lamb in its first year without blemish as a burnt offering, one ewe lamb in its first year without blemish as a sin offering, one ram without blemish as a peace offering,
15 a basket of unleavened bread, cakes of fine flour mixed with oil, unleavened wafers anointed with oil, and their grain offering with their drink offerings.
16 Then the priest shall bring them before Yahweh and offer his sin offering and his burnt offering;
17 and he shall offer the ram as a sacrifice of a peace offering to Yahweh, with the basket of unleavened bread; the priest shall also offer its grain offering and its drink offering.
18 Then the Nazirite shall shave his consecrated head at the door of the tabernacle of meeting, and shall take the hair from his consecrated head and

put it on the fire which is under the sacrifice of the peace offering.

If we realize that the term *go up* means *to go up to Jerusalem*, then we can see that Shaul did go up to Jerusalem after he separated his Nazirite vow.

Ma'asei (Acts) 18:21-22
21 But he took leave of them, saying, "By all means it is necessary for me to keep the coming feast in Jerusalem: But I will come again to you, Elohim willing!"
22 And when he had landed at Caesarea, and gone up [to Jerusalem] and greeted the ecclesia, he went down to Antioch.

Shaul separated yet another Nazirite vow when he met with the apostles in Acts 21. While those in Jerusalem were elated to hear of Shaul's successes among the gentiles, they had heard rumors that Shaul was no longer zealous for the Torah of Moshe (as they were)— and they had even heard rumors that Shaul now taught *against* the Torah of Moshe. Let's read carefully, and try to visualize the conversation.

Ma'asei (Acts) 21:20-22
20 And when they heard it, they glorified Yahweh. And they said to him, "Behold, brother, how many myriads of Jews there are who have believed, and they are all zealous for the Torah [of Moshe]!
21 But they have been informed about you that you teach all the Jews who are among the Gentiles to forsake [the Torah of] Moshe, saying that they ought not to circumcise their children, nor to walk according to the [Hebraic] customs.

22 What then [is the truth]? The assembly must certainly meet [because it is a pilgrimage festival], and they will hear that you have come."

Israel can be operationally defined as those believers who diligently strive to keep Yahweh's Torah—and if Shaul taught against the Torah, it would have been an offense worthy of instant disfellowship. This would be a real crisis, for Jews were coming up to Jerusalem from all over the known world to keep the Pentecost. When the assembly met, they would surely hear that Shaul was there—and if he was found to be teaching against the Torah, then the myriads of Jews who were "zealous for the Torah" (Acts 21:20, above) would want to put him out of the assembly (perhaps even by stoning).

So what could they do to dispel the misunderstandings of Shaul's epistles? Ya'akov (Jacob) had a plan. Since Shaul had come up to Jerusalem to separate his Nazirite vow, Ya'akov told him to take four other men who had also separated Nazirite vows, and pay for all of their expenses. This would be a total of fifteen animal sacrifices, which would cost a huge sum of money back in the first century. No one would pay for fifteen animal sacrifices if he did not believe in keeping the Torah—and this would show the world that Shaul also walked orderly, keeping the Torah of Moshe.

Ma'asei (Acts) 21:23-24
23 "Therefore do what we tell you: We have four men who have [also] taken a [Nazirite] vow.
24 Take them, and be purified with them, and [you] pay their expenses so that they may shave their heads—and that all may know that those things of which they were informed concerning you [teaching against the Torah] are nothing, but

that you yourself also walk orderly and keep the Torah."

This event takes place near the end of Shaul's ministry, after most of his epistles were already written. If he had really believed that the Torah and the animal sacrifices were abolished, then why did he even have a Nazirite vow? And why did he agree to pay a total of fifteen animal sacrifices, including five sin sacrifices, so that all would know that the rumors concerning him were false—and that he himself also walked orderly, and kept the Torah?

The apostles clearly continued to offer animal sacrifices after Yeshua's sacrifice. In fact, it seems to suggest that the only reason they stopped is because the Romans destroyed the temple. But many people have a strong reaction to this. They want to know why the apostles would continue to offer animal sacrifices after Yeshua's sacrifice.

We discuss the animal sacrificial system in more detail in "About Sacrifices" (in *Nazarene Scripture Studies, Volume 1*), but since it is such a critical topic, we will give a brief explanation of it here. First let us look at Hebrews 10:3-4, which tells us that it is impossible for the blood of bulls and goats to take away sins.

> Ivrim (Hebrews) 10:3-4
> 3 But in these offerings is a reminder of sins year by year;
> 4 For it is impossible for blood of bulls and goats to take away sins.

The church uses this as an alleged proof-text that the animal sacrifices are done away with—while the truth is the exact opposite.

Israel can be operationally defined as those persons who strive to keep His covenant. Those not striving to keep His covenant were always to be put outside the camp, so that the rest of the camp could be kept pure, untainted, and set apart from the defiling attitudes of the world. Whenever an Israelite became aware that he had sinned, it was always expected that he would be eager to correct himself. This stands in contrast to the judicial systems of all the other nations of the world, which are only able to maintain a false sense of law and order by means of threats of punishment.

A bride who loves her husband never needs to be punished. As soon as she realizes she is not pleasing her husband, she is eager to change (because she wants to please him). This is the same principle upon which Israel was always supposed to operate. Because of this, the sin sacrifices were never intended to take away sin. They were only intended to serve as a gruesome and expensive reminder that the wages of sin is death—and that one had to be careful to obey the marital covenant, or else one would be cut off from eternal life (as Yahweh has no reason to save those who are not diligently striving to obey His instructions).

Even though Yahweh forgives unintentional sin, He still wants a sin offering. However, if one does anything "presumptuously" (i.e., on purpose, or rebelliously), he is to be cut off from among the people.

Bemidbar (Numbers) 15:27-30
27 "And if a person sins unintentionally, then he shall bring a female goat in its first year as a sin offering.
28 So the priest shall make atonement for the person who sins unintentionally, when he sins

unintentionally before Yahweh, to make atonement for him; and it shall be forgiven him.

29 You shall have one Torah for him who sins unintentionally, for him who is native-born among the children of Israel and for the stranger who dwells among them.

30 But the person who does anything presumptuously, whether he is native-born or a stranger, that one brings reproach on Yahweh, and he shall be cut off from among his people."

King David's infamous sin with Bathsheba was both intentional and premeditated; however, King David was in denial of his sin. When the prophet Nathan helped King David realize his sin, King David immediately repented, and Yahweh forgave his sin in that moment.

> Shemuel Bet (2 Samuel) 12:13-14
> 13 So David said to Nathan, "I have sinned against Yahweh." And Nathan said to David, "Yahweh also has put away your sin; you shall not die.
> 14 However, because by this deed you have given great occasion to the enemies of Yahweh to blaspheme, the child also who is born to you shall surely die."

King David repented, and Nathan immediately told him that Yahweh had put his sin away—yet there still had to be a penalty for sin (in this case, the child of his illicit liaison with Bathsheba had to die). The death of his child served as an awful reminder that the wages of sin is death—which is why Hebrews 10:3 (above) tells us that the animal sacrifices only serve as a *reminder* of sins year by year—for the blood of bulls and goats can never take away sins. Only Yeshua could do that.

As long as a clean temple stood, the apostles offered animal sacrifices as a gruesome and costly *reminder* of their sins—and yet they still needed to accept Yeshua's ultimate atoning sacrifice, which took place when He took all our curses upon Himself, hanging upon a tree.

We explain the sacrifices in more detail in *Nazarene Scripture Studies, Volume 1*, but Acts 21 shows us that as long as the temple stood, the apostles still offered animal sacrifices at the appropriate times. This is surely because they knew Yeshua's words at Matthew 5:17 to be true—that until heaven and earth pass away, not even the smallest part of the Torah will fall away—because it is a marital covenant.

The Calendar the Apostles Kept

The Roman Church uses the Roman calendar, in which the day begins at midnight. In contrast, the Hebrew day begins at evening. For example, Genesis 1:31 tells us:

B'reisheet (Genesis) 1:31
31 And the evening and the morning were the sixth day.

Leviticus 23 verifies this, telling us that the Hebrew day lasts from evening to evening.

Vayiqra (Leviticus) 23:32
32 "On the ninth day of the month, at evening, from evening to evening, you shall observe your Sabbath."

The Roman Church justifies their worship on Sunday, Christmas, and Easter by misquoting certain passages in the Renewed Covenant (New Testament). One such passage is Acts 20:7-12.

Ma'asei (Acts) 20:7-12
7 Now on the first day of the week, when the disciples came together to break bread, Shaul, ready to depart the next day, spoke to them and continued his message until midnight.
8 There were many lamps in the upper room where they were gathered together.
9 And in a window sat a certain young man named Eutychus who was sinking into a deep sleep. He was overcome by sleep; and as Shaul continued speaking, he fell down from the third story and was taken up dead.

10 But Shaul went down, fell on him, and embracing him said, "Do not trouble yourselves, for his life is in him."

11 Now when he had come up, had broken bread and eaten, and talked a long while, even till daybreak, he departed.

12 And they brought the young man in alive, and they were not a little comforted.

According to the church, the disciples met on Sunday morning for breakfast, listened to Shaul (Paul) until midnight (when Eutychus fell out the window), ate a meal after midnight, and then continued their meeting until daybreak (Monday). This might sound like it makes sense, until we ask why there were so many lamps in the upper room during daylight hours, as well as why they skipped lunch and dinner.

In contrast, if we realize the apostles still kept the original Hebrew calendar, suddenly everything makes sense. Jewish custom is to worship at the synagogue (or at the temple) on the Sabbath, and then to meet at a friend's house after sundown. When gathering for this after-Sabbath festivity, the Jewish people usually share a communal meal. This is called *breaking bread*. If the disciples gathered after the Sabbath ended (just after sundown) and ate a communal dinner together, this would explain why they needed so many lamps. It would also make it clear that they were enjoying a traditional Jewish time of worship and celebration.

This same kind of post-Sabbath fellowship is also recorded in the book of John.

Yochanan (John) 20:19
19 Then, the same day at evening, being the first day of the week, when the doors were shut where

the disciples were assembled, for fear of the [Orthodox] Jews, Yeshua came and stood in the midst, and said to them, "Peace be with you."

Yeshua was put to death at the spring festival of the Passover. Jerusalem can already be hot then—and if it was hot, the logical thing would have been to leave the doors open. However, since there was persecution, the disciples closed their doors.

Why should the Christian Church use these passages to justify Sunday worship, when the book of Acts says the Apostle Shaul's custom was to go into the Jewish synagogues on the Sabbath?

Ma'asei (Acts) 13:14-16
14 But going through from Perga, they arrived to Antioch-Pisidia, and going into the synagogue on the day of the Sabbath, they sat down.
15 And after the reading of the Torah and of the Prophets, the synagogue rulers sent to them, saying, "Men, brothers, if there is any word of exhortation to the people, speak!"
16 And rising up and signaling with his hand, Shaul said, "Men, Israelites, and the ones fearing Elohim, hear!"

The church teaches that Shaul went throughout the known world, pulling Jews out of the synagogues, and planting Sunday churches. But how do they support this claim? Shaul did start a new assembly when he got thrown out of the (Pharisaic) synagogue in Corinth, and he established a Nazarene assembly next door—but they also met on the Sabbath.

Ma'asei (Acts) 18:5-8

5 When Silas and Timothy had come from Macedonia, Shaul was compelled by the Spirit, and testified to the Jews that Yeshua is the Messiah.

6 But when they opposed him and blasphemed, he shook his garments and said to them, "Your blood be upon your own heads; I am clean. From now on I will go to the Gentiles."

7 And he departed from there and entered the house of a certain man named Justus, one who worshiped Elohim, whose house was next door to the synagogue.

8 Then Crispus, the ruler of the synagogue, believed on Yahweh with all his household. And many of the Corinthians, hearing, believed and were immersed [baptized].

Although Shaul founded a new assembly at Corinth, it would not have been called a "church"—it was probably called a synagogue, or a kehillah (assembly). More importantly, this assembly met on the Sabbath, just like the Nazarene they followed had done.

Luqa (Luke) 4:16
16 So (Yeshua) came to Nazareth, where He had been brought up. And, as His custom was, He went into the synagogue on the Sabbath day, and stood up to read.

The King James Version (KJV) uses the word *Easter* in Acts 12:4, simply because the King James translators incorrectly rendered the Greek word *Pascha* (Passover) as "Easter."

Ma'asei (Acts) 12:4
4 And when he had apprehended him, he put him in prison, and delivered him to four quaternions of

soldiers to keep him; intending after Easter (sic) to bring him forth to the people.

All major versions since the King James Version have since corrected this error.

There are several other references to the Passover in the Renewed Covenant. All these demonstrate that the apostles were still keeping the Hebrew calendar even many years after Yeshua's ascension.

> Ma'asei (Acts) 20:6
> 6 And we sailed away after the Days of Unleavened Bread [i.e., Passover].

Numerous references also tell us that the apostles continued to observe the Pentecost.

> Qorintim Aleph (1 Corinthians) 16:8
> 8 But I will remain in Ephesus until Pentecost.

This was still Pentecost on the Hebrew calendar, because Shaul was hurrying to observe this festival in Jerusalem (rather than Rome).

Ma'asei (Acts) 20:16
16 For Shaul had decided to sail by Ephesus, so as not to spend time in Asia, for he hastened if it was possible for him to be in Jerusalem on the day of Pentecost.

The apostles also kept the Day of Atonement at Acts 27:9. It is here called "the Fast," because the Jews traditionally observe it by fasting.

Ma'asei (Acts) 27:9

9 And much time having passed, and the voyage already being dangerous because the Fast had now gone by....

Even though the word "Fast" is translated perfectly from Greek to English, one can easily miss the fact that the apostles were still using the Hebrew calendar, if one does not realize the apostles were writing in the vernacular.

It is not okay to change the calendar like this, because the calendar is part of the Torah—and Yeshua said not to think he had come to destroy either the Torah, or the Prophets.

> Mattityahu (Matthew) 5:17-19
> 17 "Do not think that I came to destroy the Torah, or the Prophets. I did not come to destroy [them], but [only] to fulfill them.
> 18 For truly, I say to you, till heaven and earth pass away, nothing at all will pass from the Law, until all is fulfilled.
> 19 Whoever therefore breaks one of the least of these commandments, and teaches men so, shall be called least in the kingdom of heaven; but whoever does and teaches them, he shall be called great in the kingdom of heaven."

Yet while Yeshua clearly said not to think He came to destroy the Torah or the Prophets, many Christians believe He did just that. They say that because He kept the festivals, He *fulfilled* the festivals, and therefore the feasts are now done away with. But if you find your marriage fulfilling, does that mean it is now done away with? That does not even make sense.

There are other problems with the Christian version. In Luke 4:18, Yeshua stood up in the synagogue and said He had come to fulfill the first part of the prophecies in Isaiah 61.

Luqa (Luke) 4:16-19
16 So He came to Nazareth, where He had been brought up. And as His custom was, He went into the synagogue on the Sabbath day, and stood up to read.
17 And He was handed the book of the prophet Yeshayahu (Isaiah). And when He had opened the book, He found the place where it was written:
18 "The Spirit of Yahweh is upon Me, because He has anointed Me to preach the Good News to the poor. He has sent Me to heal the brokenhearted, to proclaim liberty to the captives and recovery of sight to the blind, to set at liberty those who are oppressed, and
19 "to proclaim the acceptable year of Yahweh…."

However, He stopped short of saying that He had come to fulfill the Day of Vengeance. The part He has not fulfilled yet is in Isaiah 61:2.

Yeshayahu (Isaiah) 61:2
2 And the Day of Vengeance of our Elohim.

So if Yeshua came to fulfill the first part of Isaiah 60-61, will He never fulfill the second part? Also, what about the rest of the prophecies, and the Torah?

The Torah and Prophets all speak of Yeshua's return— but if the Torah and the Prophets are now destroyed (as the Christians say), then how will He return for His bride?

If the Christians are right, and the Torah and the Prophets were annulled, then why does Shaul tell us that the festivals are prophetic shadows of things still to come? That is what Colossians 2:16-17 says, although most people do not realize it because of errors in most English translations. For example, the KJV supplies two words (*days*, and *is*) in italics:

Colossians 2:16-17, KJV
16 Let no man therefore judge you in meat, or in drink, or in respect of an holy day, or of the new moons, or of the sabbath *days*:
17 Which are a shadow of things to come; but the body *is* of Christ.

With the addition of these two italicized words, the KJV makes it sound like we should never let a brother judge us according to what we eat or drink, or what days we keep for worship. It makes it sound like it makes no difference whether we keep the same days of worship the apostles kept, or whether we keep Sunday, Easter, Christmas, Ramadan, or the Chinese New Year, because (after all) the body is _of_ Messiah. However, Scripture tells us we are not supposed to add or take away from His words—and that if we change His words, then we are not obeying His commandments, but our own. For example,

Devarim (Deuteronomy) 4:2
2 "You shall not add to the word which I command you, nor take from it, that you may keep the commandments of Yahweh your Elohim, which I command you."

Since we are not supposed to add to His word, let's take the words *days* and *is* back out, and see what

58

difference it makes. Here is the same passage with those two words omitted.

Colossians 2:16-17 (KJV, no added words)
16 Let no man therefore judge you in meat, or in drink, or in respect of an holy day, or of the new moons, or of the sabbath; which are a shadow of things to come; but the Body of Christ.

If we read this passage closely, we will see that there are three main ideas mentioned here (1-2-3):

1. Let no man therefore judge you in meat, or in drink, or in respect of an holy day, or of the new moons, or of the Sabbath
2. which are a [prophetic] shadow of things [still] to come
3. but the Body of [Messiah]

If we rearrange the clauses to make the English read better (3-1-2), we find that Shaul really said to let the body of Messiah judge us in meat, in drink, or in respect of a Sabbath or festival day, because the festivals are prophetic shadow pictures of things still to come.

Qolossim (Colossians) 2:16-17 (Re-ordered)
16 Let no man but the Body of Messiah judge you in meat, or in drink, or in respect of an holy day, or of the new moons, or of the Sabbath; for the festivals are shadows of things [still] to come.

Rather than telling us that the festivals do not matter anymore (and that we can do what we want), Shaul is actually saying that we should keep the Sabbath, the festivals, and the new moon days, because they are prophetic shadows of future events. This meaning is not at all reflected in the New International Version (NIV), which reads:

Colossians 2:16-17, NIV
16 Therefore do not let anyone judge you by what you eat or drink, or with regard to a religious festival, a New Moon celebration or a Sabbath day.
17 These are a shadow of the things that were to come; the reality, however, is found in Christ.

The NIV says that these prophetic shadows of future events are all irrelevant now because they were only shadows of things that "were to come." It seems to suggest that Messiah's coming did away with all of these things—so as long as we believe Yeshua is the Messiah, it makes no difference what we eat and drink, or what days of worship we decide to keep (if any). But what sense does this make? The apostles had to be in Jerusalem during the feast of the Pentecost on the appointed time, so they could receive the outpouring of the Set apart Spirit.

Ma'asei (Acts) 2:1-2
1 And in the fulfilling of the Day of Pentecost, they [the faithful] were all with one mind, in one place.
2 And suddenly there came a sound from heaven, as of a rushing mighty wind, and it filled the whole house where they were sitting.

Christian theologians say that the Torah and the Prophets were not abolished immediately. They say that Yeshua's death ushered in a 300-400 year time of transition in which the church fathers had Yahweh's permission to make any changes they wanted to the faith—changes which Yahweh had never prophesied, and which are in complete contradiction to Scripture.

Amos 3:7
7 Surely Yahweh Elohim does nothing, Unless He reveals His secret to His servants the prophets.

The prophecies say nothing about Yahweh changing the festival days, which is why the apostles were still keeping them. They knew the festival days were prophetic shadow pictures of things still to come. For example, when the Spirit was poured out in Acts 2, this was a prophetic fulfillment of the giving of the Torah at Mount Sinai—and since Shaul wrote Colossians 2:16-17 after the outpouring in Acts 2 took place, we know that there will be other prophetic fulfillments as well.

While some prophecies are fulfilled only once (such as Yeshua's birth), others can have multiple fulfillments. This pattern of repeat fulfillments is easily seen in the example of the Feast of Tabernacles, also called the Feast of Booths, or Sukkot. This was fulfilled when the Israelites dwelt in tabernacles (or booths) in the Sinai wilderness, and then it was fulfilled again when Yeshua was born. While the Christians tell us Yeshua was born on December 25, the truth is that He was born on the first day of the fall Feast of Tabernacles, which is why John tells us:

Yochanan (John) 1:14
14 And the Word became flesh, and tabernacled among us.

Other versions read "and pitched His tent among us," which gives essentially the same meaning.

Christianity teaches that Yeshua was born in a manger on December 25, with donkeys and horses looking on. They claim He was swaddled and laid in a crib of hay. As romantic as this version sounds, it is far from the truth. Since Christianity does not value the Hebrew language, most Christians do not realize that in Hebrew, the word for a manger is the same as the word for a tabernacle, booth, or stall. Thus, the account of Yeshua's birth actually tells us that He was laid in a tabernacle.

Luqa (Luke) 2:7
7 And she brought forth her firstborn Son, and wrapped Him in swaddling cloths, and laid Him in a tabernacle, because there was no room for them in the inn.

Yeshua's parents had come up to Jerusalem for the pilgrimage festival, in keeping with the command.

Vayiqra (Leviticus) 23:41-43
41 You shall keep it as a feast to Yahweh for seven days in the year. It shall be a statute forever in your generations. You shall celebrate it in the seventh month.
42 You shall dwell in booths [tabernacles] for seven days. All who are native Israelites shall dwell in booths,
43 that your generations may know that I made the children of Israel dwell in booths when I brought them out of the land of Egypt: I am Yahweh your Elohim.

Joseph and Miriam (Mary) originally intended to stay at an inn. The rabbinical ruling in that time was the same as it is today: any person who is pregnant, old, or sick did not actually have to sleep in a tabernacle. Rather, for reasons of health and safety they could rent a room at an inn. However, Luke 2:7 tells us that there was no room at the inn, therefore Joseph and Miriam had to dwell in a tabernacle (booth/manger). All of this came to pass so that Yeshua might be born in a tabernacle on the first day of the fall Feast of Tabernacles, in prophetic fulfillment of the command.

While the church tells us that the feasts are all done away with, and that there will never be another fulfillment of the Feast of Tabernacles, Scripture shows this to be a lie. There are at least two more prophetic fulfillments of the Feast of Tabernacles.

> Zecharyah (Zechariah) 14:16-17
> 16 And it shall be, everyone who is left from all the nations which came up against Jerusalem shall go up from year to year to worship the King, Yahweh of hosts; and to keep the Feast of Tabernacles.
> 17 And it shall be, whoever will not go up from the families of the earth to worship the King, Yahweh of hosts, there shall even be no rain on them.

A fourth fulfillment is also prophesied in Revelation.

> Hitgalut (Revelation) 21:3
> 3 And I heard a great voice out of Heaven, saying, "Behold, the Tabernacle of Elohim is with men!" And He will tabernacle with them, and they will be His peoples, and Elohim Himself will be their Elohim.

In contrast, the church tells us "Jesus" was born on December 25. However, this is a pagan Roman festival day called Saturnalia (Bacchanalia). It takes place four days after the winter solstice, in honor of the rebirth of the sun. The gods Saturn and Jupiter are alternate names for Lucifer, so December 25 is essentially Satan's birthday in disguise.

The Roman Church renamed Saturnalia in honor of the Messiah, but Yahweh warns us not to honor Him with the things of the pagans, or to add or take away anything at all from the covenant that He gave.

Devarim (Deuteronomy) 12:30-32
30 "Take heed to yourself that you are not ensnared to follow them, after they are destroyed from before you, and that you do not inquire after their gods, saying, 'How did these nations serve their gods? I also will do likewise.'
31 You shall not worship Yahweh your Elohim in that way; for every abomination to Yahweh which He hates they have done to their gods; for they burn even their sons and daughters in the fire to their gods.
32 Whatever I command you, be careful to observe it; you shall not add to it nor take away from it."

If the apostles had kept Christmas on December 25, it would have been recorded in Acts. However, the word *Christmas* is not found anywhere in Scripture. Further, December is not a month in the Hebrew calendar, so why would the apostles have kept a pagan festival?

Yeshua tells us that He went to prepare a place for His bride in His Father's house.

Yochanan (John) 14:2-3
2 "In My Father's house are many mansions; if it were not so, I would have told you.
I go to prepare a place for you.

3 And if I go and prepare a place for you, I will come again and receive you to Myself; that where I am, there you may be also."

If Yeshua is a good son, and He wants to honor His Father, why would He even consider taking a *Christian* bride who worships on pagan festival days which His Father always said not to keep?

Why indeed, when there are Nazarene maidens He could marry, who *do* keep His Father's commands?

The Church: Stepping Stones

The relationship between the church and Nazarene Israel is complex. Later in this book we will show that the church fulfills the prophecies over Mystery Babylon, who is also described as the *harlot* (Revelation 17). She is a harlot because she does not have a marriage covenant (the Torah).

In Scripture, many things are a "double-edged sword" that cuts both ways. On one hand, the Christians are His people—and on the other hand, the Christians are *not* His people (at least not in the fullest sense). It takes a good bit of spiritual maturity to see the Christians for who they are, and to love them (rather than condemn them)—for it is only by loving anyone (the Christians, the Jews, our Islamic cousins, or secular people) that we can ultimately draw them closer to the truth.

Yeshua told the woman at the well that the "true" worshippers must worship His Father not just in Spirit, but also in truth. This is an amazingly important axiom.

> Yochanan (John) 4:21-24
> 21 Yeshua said to her, "Woman, believe Me, the hour is coming when you will neither on this mountain, nor in Jerusalem, worship the Father.
> 22 You [Samaritans] worship what you do not know; we know what we worship, for salvation [literally: Yeshua] is of the Jews.
> 23 But the hour is coming, and now is, when the true worshipers will worship the Father in spirit and truth; for the Father seeks such to worship Him.

24 Elohim is Spirit, and those who worship Him must worship in spirit and in truth."

When Yeshua spoke of truth, He probably meant the definition in Scripture (which is the Torah).

Tehillim (Psalms) 119:142
142 Your righteousness is an everlasting righteousness, and Your Torah is truth.

To be true worshippers, we need to worship the Father both in the Spirit and in the Torah. If we do not worship both in the Spirit and in the Torah, then we are on the broad, easy road that leads to destruction.

Mattityahu (Matthew) 7:13-14
13 "Enter through the narrow gate; for the gate is wide and the road is easy that leads to destruction, and there are many who take it.
14 And the gate is narrow and the road is afflicted that leads to life; and there are few who find it."

It is absolutely essential to listen for the voice of the Spirit moment by moment, and walk according to it. However, only seven verses later (in the same general context), Yeshua warns us that there will be a large group of people who call Him "Lord" who will not enter into the kingdom of heaven.

Mattityahu (Matthew) 7:21-23
21 "Not everyone who says to Me, 'Lord, Lord,' shall enter the kingdom of heaven, but he who does the will of My Father in heaven.
22 Many will say to Me in that day, 'Lord, Lord, have we not prophesied in Your name, cast out demons in Your name, and done many wonders in Your name?'

23 And then I will declare to them, 'I never knew you; depart from Me, you who practice lawlessness [torahlessness]!'."

This may be hard for some to accept, but the Christians are the only group of people that fits this list of criteria. The Christians are the only group that

1. Are many
2. Call Him Lord
3. Prophesy in His name
4. Cast out demons in His name
5. Do many works of power in His name
6. Are lawless (do not keep the Torah)

What Yeshua is saying here is that even if we prophesy in His name, cast out demons in His name, and do many mighty works in His name, if we are lawless (i.e., we do not try to keep Torah), we will go to destruction because we are not trying to keep the marital covenant.

But why would Yeshua reject the Christians, when the Christians are largely responsible for spreading the Good News of Him to the four corners of the earth? As we will see in the next few chapters, Christianity is only an intermediate step in the grand multi-step plan of salvation for all mankind. It was a very important step, but still only a step. If we take one or two steps in a long journey, and then stop, we will never complete the journey—or, in this case, we will never complete the spiritual transformation. We will stop short of learning how to worship the Father both in Spirit and in truth (Torah). That means we will miss the mark.

If we say we abide in Yeshua, then we need to walk even as Yeshua walked.

Yochanan Aleph (1 John) 2:6
6 He who says he abides in Him ought himself also to walk just as He walked.

None of us will ever be perfect as Yeshua was, but it is essential that we try. We are to attempt to keep the marital covenant, walking in as much love as we can. It is essential to walk in the Spirit—but it is also essential to keep the truth/Torah.

The Nazarene faith spread more rapidly inside the land of Israel than Christianity did, because the Jews in the land understood that the Torah is a marital covenant. The Nazarenes in the land were "zealous for the Torah," as Ya'akov (James) also says.

Ma'asei (Acts) 21:20
20 And when they heard it, they glorified Yahweh. And they said to him, "You see, brother, how many myriads of Jews there are who have believed, and they are all zealous for the Torah."

Outside the land, however, it was a different story. The Hellenized Jews were not zealous for the Torah, and the gentiles did not understand that the Torah is a bridal covenant; thus it was much easier for Hellenized Jews and gentiles to accept lawless Christianity, since it promised the same eternal rewards with less work.

Even though torahless Christianity is not the original faith, it serves an important function. It makes it easier for gentiles to accept faith in a Jewish Messiah, even if they do not understand the need to keep His covenant. Christianity is therefore an imperfect vehicle which can brings the gentiles into relationship with Yeshua. Even if the relationship is not perfect, it brings them closer to Him than before.

It is essential that we understand this principle of bringing people closer, or taking them further away. When something brings people closer to Yeshua, even in an imperfect way, we tolerate it, because in the end it brings people closer to our Husband.

Marqaus (Mark) 9:38-40
38 Now Yochanan (John) answered Him, saying, "Teacher, we saw someone who does not follow us casting out demons in Your name, and we forbade him because he does not follow us."
39 But Yeshua said, "Do not forbid him, for no one who works a miracle in My name can soon afterward speak evil of Me.
40 For he who is not against us is on our side."

At the same time, when someone (usually a leader or a teacher) leads people further away from Yeshua, we have to bear in mind that they are not our friends.

Luqa (Luke) 11:23
23 "He who is not with Me is against Me, and he who does not gather with Me scatters."

This is why it is easier to love torahless Christians (who are misled) than it is to love torahless Christian leaders and teachers (who are doing the misleading). Even though the Christian leaders and teachers are misled themselves, Scripture holds them to a much higher standard.

Ya'akov (James) 3:1
3 My brethren, let not many of you become teachers, knowing that we shall receive a stricter judgment.

After the Romans exiled the Jews from the land of Israel, the Nazarenes had a much harder time. People generally follow the principle of least effort, and the torahless Christian faith was much more attractive to the gentiles and Hellenized Jews, because it promised the same reward with less effort. Therefore Christianity waxed strong, and the Nazarene faith began to wane.

As Christianity began to grow, other forces came into play that modified it. In the next chapter we will see how the Roman Emperor Constantine took torahless Christianity, and merged it with the Roman sun worship of the day to form the Catholic (Universal) Church, which was yet another transitional vehicle.

The Papacy as Anti-Messiah

Because our Jewish brethren understood that the Torah was their bridal covenant, they were unwilling to accept Christianity's premise (that they could please Yahweh without Torah). That is also why, when Shaul (Paul) went up to Jerusalem in Acts 21, Ya'akov (James) was able to point out how many believers there were in Jerusalem who were still zealous for the Torah.

Ma'asei (Acts) 21:20
20 And when they heard it, they glorified Yahweh. And they said to him, "Behold, brother, how many myriads of Jews there are who have believed, and they are all zealous for the Torah [of Moshe]!"

Outside the land of Israel, however, it was a different story. Neither the Hellenized Jews nor the gentiles understood that the Torah was a bridal covenant, therefore it was easier for them to accept the torahless version (Christianity), seeing as it promised the same rewards with less obedience. This torahless Christian variation spread rapidly outside the land of Israel, adopting pagan sun-worship practices, rituals, and idols as it went. By the year 150 CE, Sunday worship was fairly well established, as evidenced by the testimony of Justin Martyr.

But Sunday is the day on which we all hold our common assembly, because it is the first day on which God, having wrought a change in the darkness and matter, made the world; and Jesus Christ our Saviour on the same day rose from the dead. For He was crucified on the day before that of Saturn (Saturday); and on the day after that of Saturn, which is the day of the Sun, having appeared to His apostles and disciples, He taught them these things, which we have submitted to you also for your consideration.

[Justin Martyr, First Apology, Chapter 67 - Weekly Worship of the Christians, circa 150 CE, Biblesoft]

Rome controlled the Middle East in the years after Yeshua's ("Jesus'") death, and the official Roman religion was Mithraism. In Mithraism, the sun god (Ra) was thought to personally attend the Roman emperor, giving him unparalleled power and prestige. Whenever a Roman citizen came to believe in the Messiah, he no longer saw the emperor as a demigod—and this weakened his power and prestige. For this reason the Roman emperors hated the Nazarene and Christian faiths, and persecuted them both unto death. However, the more Christians and Nazarenes were killed, the more Roman citizens became aware of the Messiah, and converted to Christianity and Nazarene Israel.

Then, in the fourth century, everything changed. History tells us that in 312, the Roman Emperor Constantine was in the grove of the so-called sun god Apollo (i.e., Lucifer), in ancient France, where he claimed to have had a vision in which "Christ" appeared to him, telling him to write the first two letters of his name (XP) upon his troops' shields. This he did. Then the next day Constantine claimed to have seen a cross superimposed over the sun, at which time he was given the message, "In hoc signo vinces" ("In this sign you will be victorious")—and he went on to win many battles. [Note: the cross is an ancient sign of Tammuz, another sun god, i.e., Lucifer in another form.]

Some scholars believe Constantine did not truly convert to Christianity (at least not at first). Rather, they believe he may have converted for political reasons. At the time of Constantine's conversion, his empire was about half Christian. The other half worshipped Sol Invictus Mith-Ra (the invincible god of the sun). Perhaps Constantine reasoned that if he pretended to be a Christian, and yet worshipped on pagan days of worship, that he would be able to unify his empire?

However, let us consider an alternate hypothesis. Earlier we saw how Christians believe it is alright to worship on whatever days they want. If Constantine felt it was alright to worship on whatever festival days he wanted, he might not have had a problem worshipping on sun worship festival days. And he might not have had a problem merging sun worship rites and rituals with torahless Christianity, so long as it unified his empire.

The year after Constantine's conversion (in 312 CE), he and his then co-emperor Licinius co-issued the Edict of Milan, which technically ended the persecution of Christians within the Roman Empire. Constantine then went on to consolidate his hold on power throughout the Roman Empire, and by 324 he reigned supreme. The next year (325) he convened the Council of Nicea (or Nice), in which Mithraism and Christianity were merged to form the Catholic (Universal) faith. The Christians were pleased, since they did not care what days of worship they kept—and it also satisfied the sun worshippers, since they got to worship the same idols on the same festival days as before (only with new Christian names).

Constantine gave his new Universal (Catholic) faith eleven years to become accepted before he banned all other versions of the faith in Yeshua, including the Nazarene faith. As we saw in the first chapter, the Nazarenes were now labeled heretics for keeping the same Torah, Sabbath, and festivals as Yeshua and His apostles had kept three centuries earlier.

"The Nazarenes do not differ in any essential thing from them [the Orthodox Jews], since they practice the customs and doctrines prescribed by Jewish Law; except that they believe in Christ. They believe in the resurrection of the dead, and that the universe was created by God. They preach that God is One, and that Jesus Christ is His Son. They are very learned in the Hebrew language. They read the Law [the Law of Moses].... Therefore they differ...from the true Christians because they fulfill until now [such] Jewish rites as the circumcision, Sabbath and others."
[Epiphanius of Salamis, "Against Heresies," Panarion 29, 7, pp. 41, 402]

In the Council of Laodicea (in 336), Constantine ruled that if anyone was found "Judaizing" (i.e., keeping the original Nazarene faith), he should be "shut out from [the body of] Christ."

Christians must not Judaize by resting on the Sabbath; but must work on that day, honoring rather the Lord's Day [Sunday] by resting, if possible, as Christians. However, if any [Nazarene] be found Judaizing, let them be shut out from Christ. [The Church of Rome; Council of Laodicea under the Emperor Constantine; Canon 29, 336 CE]

This phrase can also be translated as *Let them be anathema to Christ*, which meant it was okay to kill them for not keeping the new mixed worship. Since history repeats itself, and since the coming one world religion will be formed around the papacy, we can expect to see this pattern again.

Who, then, is the pope? In 2 Thessalonians, Shaul warned that a coming "man of sin" would sit in a coming temple, pretending to be Elohim Himself.

> Thessaloniqim Bet (2 Thessalonians) 2:3-4
> 3 Do not let anyone deceive you in any way, because that Day will not come unless first comes the falling away, and the man of sin is revealed, the son of perdition,
> 4 the one opposing and exalting himself over everything being called Elohim, or object of worship, so as for him to sit in the temple of Elohim as Elohim, showing himself that he is Elohim.

1 John 3:4 tells us that sin is the transgression of the law. Therefore, the man of sin in verse 3 might well be called the man of lawlessness/torahlessness—and who has done more to teach against the Torah, than the pope?

> Thessaloniqim Bet (2 Thessalonians) 2:7-8
> 7 For the mystery of lawlessness is already at work; only he is holding back now, until it comes out of the midst;
> 8 and then the lawless one will be revealed, whom Yahweh will consume by the spirit of His mouth, and destroy with the brightness of His coming.

When Shaul prophesied this in the first century, the lawless/torahless one had not yet been revealed (which is why this prophecy is in the future tense). However, today the lawless one has been in power for some 1,700 years. He is the "little horn" of Daniel 7, who has eyes and a mouth, speaks pompous words, and wages war against the saints, whose appearance is greater than his fellows.

Daniel 7:19-21
19 "Then I wished to know the truth about the fourth beast, which was different from all the others, exceedingly dreadful, with its teeth of iron and its nails of bronze, which devoured, broke in pieces, and trampled the residue with its feet;
20 and the ten horns that were on its head, and the other horn which came up, before which three fell, namely, that horn which had eyes and a mouth which spoke pompous words, whose appearance was greater than his fellows.
21 I was watching; and the same horn was making war against the saints, and prevailing against them."

The pope sits in a type of temple, showing himself as Elohim, and he has attempted to change the appointed feast times and the Torah (and will attempt to do so again).

Daniel 7:25
25 "And he [pope] shall speak words against [i.e., contrary to the words of] the Most High; and shall wear out the saints of the Most High; and he intends to change the appointed [festival] times and Torah. And they [saints] shall be given into his hand for a time, and times, and half a time."

The "time, times, and half a time" correspond to 3 1/2 prophetic years. The Hebrew calendar year is 360 days long. When one multiplies these 360 days times the 3 1/2 prophetic years, one gets 1,260 prophetic days. But how can we interpret this? Ezekiel 4 tells us that a prophetic day can equal an earth year.

Yehezqel (Ezekiel) 4:6
6 "And when you have completed them, lie again on your right side; then you shall bear the iniquity of the house of Judah forty days. I have laid on you a day for each year."

If the 1,260 prophetic days correspond to 1,260 earth years, then the reference to the saints being given into the papacy's hand for "a time, and times, and half a time" refers to a time period of about 1,260 years. This does not have to be fulfilled with split-second precision, but is rather a prophetic time window that stretches from the formation of the Roman church dogma (late in the third century) until the Protestant Reformation in 1519 CE. It also corresponds to the 1,260 year span between the establishment of Catholic doctrine (circa 325-330 CE), and the sinking of the (Catholic) Spanish Armada by the Protestant English navy in 1588 CE. The dates do not have to be exact, because these refer to moves of the Spirit.

We also need to understand that the Greek term *anti* does not mean *against*. Rather, it means *in place of* (or *instead of*). An anti-Messiah, therefore, is not a man who fights against the Messiah, but a man who pretends to be the Messiah. Interestingly, one of the pope's titles is *Vicarius Philii Dei*, which means *instead of the Son of the Deity*, or, *in place of the Son of the Deity*. This title comes from a document called the Donation of Constantine, which granted the pope authority over the western leg of the Roman Empire. Even though the document was later shown to be forged, a great many Catholics still refer to the pope as the Vicar of Christ (i.e., he who stands in for the Messiah). This title has further significance when we realize that Latin assigns numerical values to its letters, and when one adds up the numerical values of the letters of *Vicarious Philii Dei*, one gets a numerical value of 666, which Revelation tells us is the number of the beast.

Hitgalut (Revelation) 13:18
18 "Here is wisdom: Let the one having reason count the number of the beast, for it is the number of a man, and its number is 666."

In *Revelation and the End Times* we show how Islam also fulfills this prophecy, and how Islam works in tandem with the papacy. However, the papacy came first, and is therefore in the lead role.

In Daniel 7:25 (above) we saw that the pope would attempt to change the appointed festival times and the Torah. This is strictly against the Torah, which tells us not to add or take anything away from Yahweh's words.

Devarim (Deuteronomy) 12:32
32 "Whatever I command you, be careful to observe it; you shall not add to it nor take away from it."

The pope also calls himself the Holy Father, which Yeshua expressly forbids because that title belongs to His Father Yahweh.

Mattityahu (Matthew) 23:8-9

8 "But you, do not be called 'Rabbi'; for One is your Teacher: the Messiah; and you are all brethren.
9 And call no one on earth your 'Father', for One is your Father; the One in heaven."

If we are willing to receive it, the papacy is simply the Renewed Covenant (New Testament) antitype of the serpent in the Garden of Eden. The book of Genesis is considered prophetic, and it sets the pattern for events that occur later. Back in the Garden, the adversary appeared to Havvah (Eve) and tried to get her to disobey Yahweh's voice, telling her that there would not be any consequences for disobedience.

B'reisheet (Genesis) 3:1-3
1 Now the serpent was more cunning than any beast of the field which Yahweh Elohim had made. And he said to the woman, "Has Elohim indeed said, 'You shall not eat of every tree of the garden'?"
2 And the woman said to the serpent, "We may eat the fruit of the trees of the garden;
3 but of the fruit of the tree which is in the midst of the garden, Elohim has said, 'You shall not eat it, nor shall you touch it, lest you die.'"

The pope says essentially the same thing—that we can disregard the marital covenant, and still inherit eternal life.

The papacy says that we do not need to obey Elohim's commandments, since we are capable of knowing for ourselves what is good and what is evil.

B'reisheet (Genesis) 3:4

4 Then the serpent said to the woman, "You will not surely die,
5 for Elohim knows that in the day you eat of it your eyes will be opened, and you will be like Elohim, knowing good and evil."

The Two Houses of Israel

Have you ever wondered why the United States has a special relationship with Great Britain, and also with Israel? This is explained by the Two House Theory. This theory is so important that we will come back to it repeatedly through the balance of this book.

Genesis is prophetic. It establishes patterns that are repeated throughout Scripture. For example, when Adam and Havvah (Eve) disobeyed Yahweh, they fell from His favor (grace) and could no longer live in His land. This was the prophetic foreshadow.

Israel had twelve sons, who fathered the twelve tribes of Israel. We will soon see how the ten northern tribes disobeyed Yahweh's Torah, and thereby fell from His favor, and (like Adam and Havvah) had to leave His land. Therefore, Yahweh sent the Assyrians to take the ten northern tribes out of His land, and scatter them in what is today called Syria and Iraq. This was one prophetic fulfillment of the prophetic foreshadow.

The two southern tribes (Judah and Benjamin) were more obedient to the Torah, so Yahweh left them in the land at the time of the Assyrian invasions. Over time, these two remaining tribes came to be called simply *the Jews*. In the first century the Jews fell from Yahweh's favor because they rejected Yeshua as the Messiah. That is why Yahweh could no longer allow them to live in the land, and He had the Romans exile them. This was another fulfillment.

The exiled ten northern tribes eventually forgot about Yahweh and the Torah, and they intermarried with the

Assyrian people. When the Assyrian empire fell, it was conquered by several nations from all different directions. The conquerors to the north and west of the old Assyrian Empire, however, showed classic Israelite behaviors and characteristics, and began to be more successful militarily. They were also more prosperous, and they showed greater technological innovation. (This can only be explained in spiritual terms. We will see later how these are all blessings that Yahweh promises to His people.)

In turn, when the empires that conquered Assyria broke up, the pattern repeated itself. The empires to the north and west developed stronger economies. They had greater technological innovation, and had more military prowess. The ten northern tribes were migrating, so to speak, by an unseen spiritual process.

This invisible spiritual migration continued through the centuries, but when it reached northwestern Europe, there was no place left to go, so the migrations halted temporarily. Centuries later, northwestern Europe underwent the Protestant Reformation. Because the Protestants began seeking Yahweh's face directly, and began reading Yahweh's word themselves, Yahweh blessed the Protestant people, making them the richest, the most militarily successful, and the most technologically advanced people on earth.

Even while Yahweh was blessing the European Protestants, there was a spiritual split as Protestant separatists chose to migrate to the New World in order to escape persecution by the state-run churches of Europe. They wanted to worship Yahweh according to their understanding of Scripture (rather than as their state-run churches said to do). The United States is one of the nations where Yahweh's faithful went to seek religious freedom in Him, and it would eventually become the richest, most militarily successful, and most technologically advanced nation on earth. This was a blessing that came from Yahweh.

Let us realize that the Two House Theory does not favor any one race over another. It merely shows how Yahweh historically used the European peoples to spread the Good News of His Son around the world. It does not suggest any ultimate genetic superiority. In fact, today the greatest rise in Protestantism is taking place in Asia, and in the southern hemisphere. Wherever people draw closer to Yahweh and His Son, and seek to follow His Spirit, Yahweh will send His blessings (individually or corporately).

We need to know that Scripture calls the lost ten tribes the *house of Israel,* or the *house of Ephraim.* If we understand that these terms are interchangeable, we can see some surprising things about the Messiah's ministry.

Mattityahu (Matthew) 15:24
24 But He answered and said, "I was not sent [at this time] except to the lost sheep of the house of Israel [the lost ten tribes]."

The reason most Jews did not accept Yeshua at His first coming was simply that He was not sent for them at that time. Rather, He was sent to begin a long, multiphase regathering process for the lost ten northern tribes of the house of Israel.

Yeshua established the Nazarene faith. However, as we saw earlier, the lawless Christian counterpart was also active in Yeshua's day (and in the apostles' time). This lawless Christian variation adopted sun-worship festivals, and then Roman Emperor Constantine mixed Mithraic rites and rituals with Christianity to form the Catholic (Universal) faith. Since the Catholic faith exalts the Roman emperors and popes above their brethren, the emperors and popes had an interest in spreading their substitute version of the Good News around the world—yet Yahweh even uses this for ultimate good.

We already saw that the Nazarene faith had difficulty spreading outside the land of Israel, because people were not familiar with the idea of the Torah being a marital covenant. It was much easier for the gentiles to accept the lawless Christian version of the Good News, than it was for them to accept the Torah-obedient Nazarene faith. The Christian variation was therefore able to spread the Good News of a Jewish Messiah around the world much faster than the Nazarene faith would have been able to do—if it would have been able to do it at all.

But, once the 1,260 years of oppression by the papacy were over and the Protestant Reformation took place, people began paying attention to Scripture, rather than the pope. Further, some of them began seeking a one-on-one relationship with the Spirit. Ironically, all of this study caused the body of Messiah to fragment; but as we will show later, Yahweh is calling a remnant of His people to come back to the original Nazarene Israelite faith, as they are led by His Spirit.

Yeshua tells us that while many are called, few are chosen.

Mattityahu (Matthew) 22:14
14 "For many are called, but few are chosen."

Scripture tells us that though the children of the house of Israel be as the sand of the sea (which can be neither numbered nor counted), only a remnant will return.

Yeshayahu (Isaiah) 10:22-23
22 For though your people, O Israel, be as the sand of the sea, A remnant of them will return; The destruction decreed shall overflow with righteousness.

If we dig deeper, we see the roots of the two houses in Genesis. Israel's eleventh child was named Joseph, and Joseph had two sons (Manasseh and Ephraim). Joseph's father Israel said that Manasseh and Ephraim would be thought of as two separate tribes (indicating that Joseph would have a double portion inheritance).

B'reisheet (Genesis) 48:5
5 "And now your two sons, Ephraim and Manasseh, who were born to you in the land of Egypt before I came to you in Egypt, are mine; as Reuben and Simeon, they shall be mine."

While the tribe of Joseph was taken away, Manasseh and Ephraim were added in their place, so instead of there being twelve tribes in Israel, now there were thirteen. However, Levi is not normally numbered among the tribes, as he was later dispersed among the tribes, to minister to them—so that brings the number back down to twelve.

When Joseph's brothers were angered by his dreams, Judah suggested he be sold into slavery in Egypt.

B'reisheet (Genesis) 37:26-27

26 So Judah said to his brothers, "What profit is there if we kill our brother and conceal his blood? 27 Come and let us sell him to the Ishmaelites, and let not our hand be upon him, for he is our brother and our flesh." And his brothers listened.

When Joseph was in Egypt, he was thrown into prison for an adultery he did not commit. This foreshadowed how our Jewish brethren would accuse the Nazarenes of idolatry (i.e., spiritual adultery) for believing on Yeshua. The Nazarenes were forced to go out into the world (which is a type of spiritual Egypt). They then took the Good News to the house of Israel (which is also called the house of Joseph).

After spending time in prison, Joseph was called before Pharaoh for his ability to interpret dreams. Because he interpreted Pharaoh's dreams correctly, and gave wise advice, Joseph was seen as wise. He was appointed to rule over all the land of Egypt, second only to Pharaoh himself. Joseph then used his power to help Pharaoh consolidate his hold on Egypt, and he was given Asenath, the daughter of the Egyptian high priest Poti-pherah, for a wife. She bore him two sons, Manasseh and Ephraim.

Genesis 1 tells us that living things reproduce after their own kinds. Since this also applies to humans, we might expect Joseph's children to be partly good Hebrews (because of Joseph), and partly spiritual pagans (because of Asenath's father, Poti-pherah). This is in fact what we see. Protestant Christians in general behave as if they are part Hebrews and part pagans, blending numerous pagan sun worship rites, rituals, and festival days into their worship.

Manasseh's name translates *he will forget his toil and his father's house.* This is a prophetic picture of England, where the Industrial Revolution began. The Industrial Revolution helped the British people (and their colonies) to forget their toil. Sadly, they also forgot their Father's house (the temple).

While both of Joseph's sons were to become great, Joseph's younger son Ephraim was to become the greater of the two.

B'reisheet (Genesis) 48:12-16
12 So Joseph brought them from beside his knees, and he bowed down with his face to the earth.
13 And Joseph took them both, Ephraim with his right hand toward Israel's left hand, and Manasseh with his left hand toward Israel's right hand, and brought them near him.
14 Then Israel stretched out his right hand and laid it on Ephraim's head, who was the younger, and his left hand on Manasseh's head, guiding his hands knowingly, for Manasseh was the firstborn.
15 And he blessed Joseph, and said:
"Elohim, before whom my fathers Abraham and Isaac walked, the Elohim who has fed me all my life long to this day,
16 the Angel who has redeemed me from all evil, bless the youths! Let my name be named upon them, and the name of my fathers Abraham and Isaac; and let them grow into a multitude in the midst of the earth."

Sometimes translators make errors. In verse 16, the phrase "grow into a multitude in the midst of the earth" is better translated as, "let them teem like a multitude of fishes in the midst of the earth."

Genesis 48:16 16 "The Angel who has redeemed me from all evil, bless the youths! Let my name be named upon them, and the name of my fathers Abraham and Isaac; and let them teem like a multitude of fishes in the midst of the earth."	(16) הַמַּלְאָךְ הַגֹּאֵל אֹתִי מִכָּל רָע יְבָרֵךְ אֶת הַנְּעָרִים וְיִקָּרֵא בָהֶם שְׁמִי וְשֵׁם אֲבֹתַי אַבְרָהָם וְיִצְחָק ǀ וְיִדְגּוּ לָרֹב בְּקֶרֶב הָאָרֶץ

In Hebrew, this kind of hint is called a *remez* (רמז). It gives us a hint at some hidden meaning. What people have grown into a multitude in the midst of the earth, and have adopted the fish as their symbol? Why, the Christian people, of course.

B'reisheet (Genesis) 48:17-19
17 Now when Joseph saw that his father [Israel] laid his right hand on the head of Ephraim, it displeased him; so he took hold of his father's hand to remove it from Ephraim's head to Manasseh's head.
18 And Joseph said to his father, "Not so, my father, for this one is the firstborn; put your right hand on his head."
19 But his father [Israel] refused and said, "I know, my son [Joseph], I know. He [Manasseh] also shall become a people, and he also shall be great; but truly his younger brother [Ephraim] shall be greater than he, and his descendants shall become a multitude of nations."

In verse 19, the phrase "multitude of nations" is *melo ha-goyim* (מְלֹא הַגּוֹיִם). This can also be translated as *fullness* or *completeness of the nations*.

Scholars have different interpretations about what *the fullness/completeness of the nations* is, but taken in context, it seems to suggest that the Ephraimite people would ultimately become a multitude of (Israelite) nations who are greater than their older brother (i.e., they are more numerous and more prosperous).

Originally settled by Protestant Christian refugees and separatists, America is richer and more populous than England. It is a "multitude of nations" in that it was first established as a union of independent states. Further, the United States is comprised of people from virtually every tribe and tongue and nation—therefore it serves as the fullness or the completeness of the nations.

In Scripture, names are always prophetic. Ephraim's name means *doubly fruitful* and *prodigious*. When we look for a Protestant Christian nation that is greater than its older brother (England), is a multitude of nations, and is doubly fruitful and prodigiously blessed, the only logical candidate is Protestant Christian America. This is why we will often refer to America as the prophetic tribe of Ephraim.

However, Ephraim can also be translated *like the dust*, meaning *extremely numerous* (everywhere). This refers to the growing body of Christians all around the world who are returning to their heritage as Israelites. In fact, we will see that Yahweh has always planned for salvation (Yeshua) to be offered to every tribe, every family, every nation, and every clan, so that many could be saved in both the east and the west.

Mattityahu (Matthew) 8:11
11 "And I say to you that many will come from east and west, and sit down with Abraham, Isaac, and Jacob in the Kingdom of Heaven."

Sometimes groups like the British Israelites and the Hebrew (Black) Israelites try to turn the Two House Theory into a racial thing. This is a mistake. Yahweh does not care what color or race we are, because Yahweh does not glory in our flesh. In fact, He does not care about our physical appearance at all—but rather, He only looks at our hearts.

Shemuel Aleph (1 Samuel) 16:7
7 But Yahweh said to Samuel, "Do not look at his [physical] appearance or at his physical stature, because I have refused him. For Yahweh does not see as man sees; for man looks at the outward appearance, but Yahweh looks at the heart."

The special relationship that exists between the US and England is a result of the brotherly sentiment that exists between Joseph's two sons, Manasseh and Ephraim. Likewise, the relationship that exists between the US and Israel is the reflection of the brotherhood between the house of Joseph (Ephraim) and the house of Judah.

The Nation Becomes Divided

After Joseph died, new kings arose who did not know of all the good things that Joseph had done for Egypt. These new kings feared Israel's children, and chose to put them to hard bondage.

After 430 years in Egypt, Yahweh sent a man named Moshe (Moses) to bring Israel's children out. He brought them through the Red (Reed) Sea to the wilderness of Sinai. Fifty days after they left Egypt, they were given the Torah at the foot of Mount Sinai. This constituted their betrothal. At that time, they were told that they would be brought into the Promised Land, the land of Canaan.

Moshe sent twelve men to spy out the land. However, only Caleb the son of Yephunneh (of the tribe of Judah) and Joshua the son of Nun (of the tribe of Ephraim) brought back a good report.

> Bemidbar (Numbers) 14:6-7
> 6 But Joshua the son of Nun and Caleb the son of Yephunneh, who were among those who had spied out the land, tore their clothes;
> 7 and they spoke to all the congregation of the children of Israel, saying: "The land we passed through to spy out is an exceedingly good land!"

It is symbolic that the two spies bringing back a good report were from the tribes of Judah and Ephraim. These two tribes represent the two houses (Judah in the south, and Ephraim in the north).

Upon Moses' death, Joshua was appointed to lead the children of Israel in the conquest of the land of Canaan. Next came the period of judges (as recorded in the book of Judges). During this time the tribes lacked strong, central leadership, and therefore the nation languished. Each man did what seemed good in his own eyes (as opposed to doing what seems good in Yahweh's eyes).

> Shophetim (Judges) 17:6
> 6 In those days there was no king in Israel; everyone did what was right in his own eyes.

After the era of the judges came the era of kings. After King Shaul's (Saul's) reign ended, King David united the children of Israel, vanquished Israel's enemies, and led them back to the marital covenant (the Torah). This established the standard for a *messiah* (anointed one), which is why David is thought of as a type of messiah (with a small *m*). One reason our Jewish brothers rejected Yeshua is that they could not see how He fits the same pattern.

As we explain in *Revelation and the End Times*, Yeshua is gathering the lost and the scattered of Israel by His Spirit for a coming battle at Armageddon (which the Ephraimites will win). After this victory they will be brought back into the covenant, and to the land of Israel. However, this gathering for the final battle is happening very slowly, over generations. Because it is taking place so slowly, our Jewish brothers could not see how He was the prophesied Messiah.

When King David died, his son Solomon reigned in his place. However, Solomon disobeyed the Torah in that he took foreign wives. Remembering that Scripture labels people by how they worship, the issue was not that his wives were foreign born. Rather, the issue was that his wives worshipped foreign gods. When Solomon wanted to please his wives, he made offerings to their false gods, and this made Yahweh angry (verse 9), and He promised to punish Solomon.

Melachim Aleph (1 Kings) 11:1-13

1 But King Solomon loved many foreign women, as well as the daughter of Pharaoh: women of the Moabites, Ammonites, Edomites, Sidonians, and Hittites —

2 from the nations of whom Yahweh had said to the children of Israel, "You shall not intermarry with them, nor they with you: [for] surely they will turn away your hearts after their gods." Solomon clung to these in love.

3 And he had seven hundred wives, princesses, and three hundred concubines; and his wives turned away his heart.

4 For it was so, when Solomon was old, that his wives turned his heart after other gods; and his heart was not loyal to Yahweh his Elohim, as was the heart of his father David.

5 For Solomon went after Ashtoreth [Easter] the goddess of the Sidonians, and after Milcom the abomination of the Ammonites.

6 Solomon did evil in the sight of Yahweh, and did not fully follow Yahweh, as did his father David.

7 Then Solomon built a high place for Chemosh the abomination of Moab, on the hill that is east of Jerusalem, and for Molech the abomination of the people of Ammon.

8 And he did likewise for all his foreign wives, who burned incense and sacrificed to their gods.

9 So Yahweh became angry with Solomon, because his heart had turned from Yahweh Elohim of Israel, who had appeared to him twice,

10 and had commanded him concerning this thing, that he should not go after other gods; but he did not keep what Yahweh had commanded.

11 Therefore Yahweh said to Solomon, "Because you have done this, and have not kept My covenant and My statutes, which I have commanded you, I will surely tear the kingdom away from you and give it to your servant.

12 Nevertheless I will not do it in your days, for the sake of your father David; [but] I will tear it out of the hand of your son.

13 However I will not tear away the whole kingdom; I will give one tribe to your son for the sake of My servant David, and [one more] for the sake of Jerusalem, which I have chosen."

Yahweh had previously promised David that Solomon would reign after him, so rather than take the reign away from the house of Judah while Solomon lived, Yahweh decided to take the reign away from the house of Judah when Solomon's son Rehoboam reigned. The reign would be given to Solomon's servant Jeroboam, of the northern house of Ephraim/Israel. Yahweh sent a prophet named Ahiyah to tell Jeroboam that he would be given rulership of the ten northern tribes. This would leave only two tribes for Solomon's son Rehoboam to rule over (Judah and Benjamin, or "the Jews").

Melachim Aleph (1 Kings) 11:29-35
29 Now it happened at that time, when Jeroboam went out of Jerusalem, that the prophet Ahiyah the Shilonite met him on the way; and he had clothed himself with a new garment; and the two were alone in the field.

30 Then Ahiyah took hold of the new garment that was on him, and tore it into twelve pieces.

31 And he said to Jeroboam, "Take for yourself ten pieces [one piece for each of the ten tribes], for thus says Yahweh the Elohim of Israel: 'Behold, I will tear the kingdom out of the hand of Solomon, and will give ten tribes to you;

32 but he [his son] shall have one tribe for the sake of My servant David, and [one more] for the sake of Jerusalem, the city which I have chosen out of all the tribes of Israel,

33 because they have forsaken Me, and worshiped Ashtoreth [Easter] the goddess of the Sidonians, Chemosh the elohim [god] of the Moabites, and Milcom the elohim [god] of the people of Ammon, and have not walked in My ways, to do what is right in My eyes, and keep My statutes and My judgments, as did his father David.

34 However, I will not take the whole kingdom out of his hand, because I have made him ruler all the days of his life for the sake of My servant David, whom I chose because he kept My commandments and My statutes.

35 But I will take the kingdom out of his son's hand and give it to you — ten tribes.'"

Yahweh had Ahiyah tell Jeroboam that He loved David because he kept His commands—and that if Jeroboam would also keep His commandments, then the house of Israel would be given to him as "an enduring house."

Melachim Aleph (1 Kings) 11:37-39
37 "So I will take you, and you shall reign over all your heart desires, and you shall be king over Israel.

38 Then it shall be, if you heed all that I command you, walk in My ways, and do what is right in My sight, to keep My statutes and My

commandments, as My servant David did, then I will be with you and build for you an enduring house, as I built for David; and will give Israel to you.

39 And I will afflict the descendants of David [the Jews] because of this, but not forever."

Yahweh promised that He would make Ephraim/Israel into the new lead house if they kept His commands. However, if they did not keep His commands/Torah they would no longer be the lead house.

In 1 Kings 12, the house of Israel rebelled against King Rehoboam, and they made Jeroboam their new king. King Jeroboam knew that he should lead the people to keep the Torah, but he had a dilemma in that the Torah tells all males to go up to Jerusalem three times a year. However, Jerusalem was in Rehoboam's territory. If the people went up to Jerusalem year upon year, eventually their loyalties would return to King Rehoboam, and they would kill him (Jeroboam).

Melachim Aleph (1 Kings) 12:26-27
26 And Jeroboam said in his heart, "Now the kingdom may return to the house of David [Judah].
27 If these people go up to offer sacrifices in the house of Yahweh at Jerusalem, then the heart of this people will turn back to their adon, Rehoboam king of Judah; and they will kill me, and go back to Rehoboam, King of Judah."

So Jeroboam came up with a plan which has several prophetic parallels to the torahless Christian church.

Melachim Aleph (1 Kings) 12:28-33

28 Therefore the king asked advice, made two calves of gold, and said to the people, "It is too much for you to go up to Jerusalem [for the festivals]. Here are your gods, O Israel, which brought you up from the land of Egypt!"
29 And he set up one in Bethel, and the other he put in Dan.
30 Now this thing became a sin, for the people went to worship before the one as far as Dan.
31 He made shrines on the high places, and made priests from every class of people, who were not of the sons of Levi.
32 Jeroboam ordained a feast on the fifteenth day of the eighth month, like the feast that was in Judah, and offered sacrifices on the altar. So he did at Bethel, sacrificing to the calves that he had made. And at Bethel he installed the priests of the high places which he had made.
33 So he made offerings on the altar which he had made at Bethel on the fifteenth day of the eighth month, in the month which he had devised in his own heart. And he ordained a feast for the children of Israel, and offered sacrifices on the altar and burned incense.

Jeroboam pushed the fall festivals back (from the seventh month to the eighth month), set up false houses of worship, and set up visible objects of worship (idols) for the people. He also made priests of anyone (not just the sons of Levi). Even though his new religious system departed from the Torah, he told the people it was legitimate.

Jeroboam's northern kingdom of Ephraim became the new lead house—but only for a time. The pattern established in the Garden of Eden is that when we obey His instructions, He blesses us and allows us to live in His land. Since they no longer obeyed the covenant, they were no longer allowed to dwell in the covenant land (because they were defiling it).

Point for point, this is the pattern the Christian church would later follow as they claimed to be the "New Israel." The church pushed the fall festivals back even further (into winter). They moved the center of worship from Jerusalem to Rome, and set up a false temple. They established idols (statuettes and graven images) within that temple, and staffed it with priests of any lineage (not just the sons of Levi). In sum, they made false feast days, made false feast sites, established a false priesthood, and set up visible objects of worship (idols).

In coming chapters we will see that Yahweh sent many prophets to tell the Ephraimites that they needed to repent, or they would be scattered to the four corners of the earth. Because they did not repent, Yahweh scattered them, just as He promised. But from those far reaches of the earth, Yahweh's Spirit will begin calling a remnant of His people back home.

Before we see how the remnant is to be gathered, let us see more about how the Ephraimites were to be scattered, for it will show us many mysteries that lie ahead.

Ephraim's Final Warnings

Yahweh loves us, and wants us to become a bride fit for His Son. He wants us to become our very best. That is why He applies high standards of discipline, like a caring drill sergeant.

In matters of discipline, Elohim is never random. Just like in the military, Elohim has a uniform code of legal justice which He applies to Himself as well as to us. And while some people might think studying matters of His Torah is being "legalistic," it behooves us to learn how Yahweh applies judgment and discipline, so we can learn how to keep out of trouble with His law.

Not only does Yahweh publish His laws, He always gives fair warning before He disciplines. He sends His servants the prophets to help people understand what horrors await them if they do not start caring about Yahweh, His feelings, and what He wants. Among the prophets Yahweh sent to the northern kingdom of Ephraim was Hoshea (Hosea).

> Hoshea (Hosea) 1:1
> 1 When Yahweh began to speak by Hosea, Yahweh said to Hosea: "Go! Take yourself a wife of harlotry, and have children of harlotry; for the land has committed great harlotry, by departing from Yahweh."

Idolatry is spiritual adultery, and because the house of Ephraim had committed idolatry/adultery with other elohim (gods), Yahweh told Hosea to take a harlot as his wife. This was to show the Ephraimites how their idolatry made Him feel.

Hoshea (Hosea) 1:3
3 So he went and took Gomer, the daughter of Diblaim, and she conceived and bore him a son.

The name Gomer means *finished*. The implication was that even Yahweh's great patience with Ephraim had finally come to an end.

Hoshea (Hosea) 1:4
4 Then Yahweh said to him: "Call his name Jezre'el, for in a little while I will avenge the bloodshed of Jezre'el on the house of Yehu [Judah], and bring an end to the kingdom of the [northern] house of Israel."

The name Jezre'el means *Elohim shall scatter*, or *Elohim will sow*, as one sows wheat into the ground. This is the concept to which Yeshua refers in some of His agricultural parables. Notice that Yahweh did not say He would destroy the Ephraimites *themselves*, He only said that He would bring an end to their *kingdom*. (We will also see references to this in the Renewed Covenant [New Testament].)

Hoshea (Hosea) 1:6
6 And she conceived again and bore a daughter. Then Elohim said to him: "Call her name Lo-Ruhamah; for I will no longer have mercy on the house of Israel; but I will utterly take them away."

Lo-Ruhamah means, *no mercy*, or *no compassion*. Yahweh was saying that He could not take any more. He was finished (Gomer) with His adulterous wife. Elohim would scatter (Jezre'el) Ephraim into the earth like wheat seed, and would no longer have compassion (Lo Ruhamah) on her because she did not care about what He wanted. No longer would Ephraim be Yahweh's people, but they would become *Lo-Ammi* (not His people).

> Hoshea (Hosea) 1:8-9
> 8 Now when she had weaned Lo-Ruhamah, she conceived and bore (another) son.
> 9 Then Elohim said: "Call his name Lo-Ammi, for you are not My people, and I will not be your Elohim."

And, yet, despite all the idolatry the Ephraimites had committed against Him, and despite the fact that they did not seem to care about Him, Yahweh was still merciful. He said He would redeem them one day, after they had repented and turned their hearts back to Him.

> Hoshea (Hosea) 1:10
> 10 "Yet the number of the children of Israel shall be as the sand of the sea, which cannot be measured or counted. And it shall be in the place where it was said to them, 'You are not My people', There it shall be said to them, 'You are sons of the living Elohim.'"

If Ephraim refused to keep the Torah, it would be like a repeat of the Garden of Eden: Yahweh would kick Ephraim out of His land, and draw out the sword after her until she repented and loved Him once again.

After many generations, Ephraim's children would be brought back to His land where they would be reunited with their Jewish brethren who would also believe on Yeshua at that time.

> Hoshea (Hosea) 1:11

11 "Then the children of Judah and the children of Israel shall be gathered together, and appoint for themselves one head; and they shall come up out of the Land, for great will be the day of Jezre'el!"

The Torah says that before a sinner can be punished, there must be two or more witnesses to his sin. Therefore, in addition to Hosea, Yahweh sent a prophet named Eliyahu (Elijah) to witness against the Ephraimites. Many Christians are familiar with Eliyahu's famous showdown with the priests of Ba'al. Very few, however, realize that the names in most Western translations have been changed. This is a big deal, because in Scripture, names are prophetic and have power.

The Creator's name (Yahweh or Yahuweh) has been altered some 6,828 times in Scripture. This is contrary to the third commandment.

Exodus 20:7 7 "You shall not take the name of Yahweh your Elohim in vain, for Yahweh will not hold him guiltless, who takes His name in vain."	(7) לֹא תִשָּׂא אֶת שֵׁם יְהוָה אֱלֹהֶיךָ לַשָּׁוְא | כִּי לֹא יְנַקֶּה יְהוָה אֵת אֲשֶׁר יִשָּׂא אֶת שְׁמוֹ לַשָּׁוְא

In Hebrew, the word *vain* is *l'shavah* (לַשָּׁוְא). This word refers to making His name *desolate* or letting it lie *useless* (i.e., bringing it to nothing). The idea here is that if we do not use His name (like He says to), we are desolating His name, and bringing it to nothing.

OT:7723 shav' (shawv); or shav (shav); from the same as OT:7722 in the sense of desolating; evil (as destructive), literally (ruin) or morally (especially guile); figuratively idolatry (as false, subjective), uselessness (as deceptive, objective; also adverbially, in vain):
KJV - false (-ly), lie, lying, vain, vanity.

For purposes of comparison, the root of the word *I'shavah* is the word *shoah*. This word refers to devastation, and it is the same word used for the Great Holocaust of World War 2.

OT:7722 show' (sho); or (feminine) show'ah (sho-aw'); or sho'ah (sho-aw'); from an unused root meaning to rush over; a tempest; by implication, devastation:
KJV - desolate (-ion), destroy, destruction, storm, wasteness.

The Orthodox rabbis tell us that we should not speak Yahweh's name, because speaking His name aloud is being disrespectful. However, while we want to be respectful, we also don't want to let His name lie desolate. We also don't want to call Him by a name that is not His own—yet that is precisely what many people do when they call Him *God* or *Lord*.

When the Roman legions conquered new lands, they allowed their formerly pagan subjects to call Elohim by the names of their false gods. This was practical, as it made it much easier for them to convert to Catholicism. Because Yahweh is also very practical, He put up with this. However, He doesn't really like it. Ultimately, He wants all of His people to learn to call Him by His true name (just as we would want people to call us by our true names, and not the names of pagan deities).

Sometimes people wonder if it is really such a big deal to call Yahweh by His real name, but He tells us it is a very big deal. It is one of the Ten Commandments that was etched into stone. Yahweh is very clear that He wants His name declared in all the earth.

Shemote (Exodus) 9:16
16 "And indeed, for this purpose I have raised you up: that I may show My power in you, and that My name may be declared in all the earth!"

Yahweh emphasizes the importance of loving Him, and knowing His true name.

Tehillim (Psalms) 91:14-16
14 "Because he has set his love upon Me, therefore I will deliver him;
I will set him on high, because he has known My name.
15 He will call upon Me, and I will answer him;
I will be with him in trouble;
I will deliver him and honor him.
16 I will satisfy Him with long life, and show him My salvation (literally: Yeshua)."

In Hebrew, Yahweh's name is spelled yod-hay-vav-hay (יהוה). There are several good theories about how to pronounce His name (*Yahweh*, *Yahuweh*, *Yahuwah*, *Yehovah*, etc.). We can accept all of these pronunciations, however, there is no way to pronounce yod-hay-vav-hay as *God* or *Lord*. When the Roman legions conquered the British Isles, they simply told the British to use these names for Yahweh, and the practice has been carried down through the centuries, even though Scripture forbids it.

We need to remember that one of Ephraim's problems is idolatry (which is spiritual adultery). When the gentiles in the British Isles were worshipping God (Gud) and Lord (Lordo/Larth), they were committing spiritual adultery. When the newly conquered pagans began worshipping Yahweh, He forgave them for having committed spiritual adultery on Him, but how do you think it made Him feel? And how does He feel now when we continue to call Him these names? How would we like it if our spouses were to commit adultery on us (Yahweh forbid!), and when they came back to us, they called us by the name of their former lovers all the time?

Many believers call Yahweh *Lord*. They think this is okay because the English have been calling Yahweh *Lord* for well over a thousand years now. In actuality, this is a fulfillment of an ancient prophetic foreshadow that took place at Eliyahu's infamous showdown with the priests of Ba'al (Lord).

1 Kings 18:17-18	(17) וַיְהִי כִּרְאוֹת
17 Then it happened, when Ahab saw Eliyahu that Ahab said to him, "Is that you, O troubler of Israel?"	אַחְאָב אֶת אֵלִיָּהוּ ׀ וַיֹּאמֶר אַחְאָב אֵלָיו הַאַתָּה זֶה עֹכֵר יִשְׂרָאֵל :
18 And he answered, "I have not troubled Israel, but you and your father's [Jeroboam's] house have, in that you have forsaken the commands of Yahweh, and have followed the Ba'als [Lords]."	(18) וַיֹּאמֶר לֹא עָכַרְתִּי אֶת יִשְׂרָאֵל כִּי אִם אַתָּה וּבֵית אָבִיךָ ׀ בַּעֲזָבְכֶם אֶת מִצְוֹת יְהוָה וַתֵּלֶךְ אַחֲרֵי הַבְּעָלִים

Notice that Eliyahu rebuked Ahab for encouraging Israel to continue in the false practices of his father, King Jeroboam. Then he challenged Ahab to gather the 450 prophets of the Lord, and the 400 prophets of Easter/Asherah/Ishtar, who eat at Jezebel's table.

Melachim Aleph (1 Kings) 18:19
19 "Now therefore, send and gather all Israel to me on Mount Carmel, the four hundred and fifty prophets of Ba'al [the Lord], and the four hundred prophets of Asherah [Easter], who eat at Jezebel's table."

Just as our forefathers forsook Yahweh for the Lord and Asherah/Ishtar/Easter, many of us do this today. Even those who know the meaning of *Lord* still call Him both *Yahweh* and *Lord* interchangeably, as if it is okay to call Yahweh by the name of a former lover.

Melachim Aleph (1 Kings) 18:20-21
20 So Ahab sent for all the children of Israel, and gathered the prophets together on Mount Carmel.
21 And Eliyahu came to all the people, and said, "How long will you keep hopping between two opinions? If Yahweh is Elohim, follow Him; but if the Lord, follow him!" But the people answered him not a word.

People are creatures of habit. Once they start calling Yahweh *Lord*, they don't like to change. Yet notice that Eliyahu makes it clear that there is a difference between *Yahweh* and *Lord*.

Melachim Aleph (1 Kings) 18:22-29

22 Then Eliyahu said to the people, "I alone am left a prophet of Yahweh; but the Lord's prophets are four hundred and fifty men!

23 Therefore let them give us two bulls; and let them choose one bull for themselves, cut it in pieces, and lay it on the wood, but put no fire under it; and I will prepare the other bull, and lay it on the wood, but put no fire under it.

24 Then you call on the name of your gods, and I will call on the name of Yahweh; and the Elohim who answers by fire, He is Elohim." So all the people answered and said, "It is well spoken."

25 Now Eliyahu said to the prophets of the Lord, "Choose one bull for yourselves and prepare it first, for you are many; and call on the name of your Elohim, but put no fire under it."

26 So they took the bull which was given them, and they prepared it, and called on the name of the Lord from morning even till noon, saying, "O Lord, hear us!" But there was no voice; no one answered. Then they leaped about the altar which they had made.

27 And so it was, at noon, that Eliyahu mocked them and said, "Cry aloud, for he is a mighty one [a god]! Either he is meditating, or he is busy, or he is on a journey; or perhaps he is sleeping, and must be awakened!"

28 So they cried aloud, and cut themselves, as was their custom, with knives and lances, until the blood gushed out on them.

29 And when midday was past, they prophesied until the time of the offering of the evening sacrifice. But there was no voice; no one answered: no one paid attention.

Yahweh gave the Ephraimite priests plenty of time to admit they were wrong. Then Eliyahu rebuilt the altar of

Yahweh that had been broken down, and he dug a trench big enough to hold two seahs of seed (probably representing the two houses of Israel). Then he had the people soak the wood with twelve jars of water.

Melachim Aleph (1 Kings) 18:30-37
30 Then Eliyahu said to all the people, "Come near to me;" so all the people came near to him. And he repaired the altar of Yahweh that was broken down.
31 And Eliyahu took twelve stones, according to the number of the tribes of the sons of Jacob, to whom the word of Yahweh had come, saying, "Israel shall be your name."
32 Then with the stones he built an altar in the name of Yahweh, and he made a trench around the altar large enough to hold two seahs of seed.
33 And he put the wood in order, cut the bull in pieces, and laid it on the wood, and said, "Fill four water-pots with water, and pour it on the burnt sacrifice and on the wood."
34 Then he said, "Do it a second time," and they did it a second time; and he said, "Do it a third time," and they did it a third time.
35 So the water ran all around the altar; and he also filled the trench with water.
36 And it came to pass, at the time of the offering of the evening sacrifice, that Eliyahu the prophet came near and said, "Yahweh, Elohim of Abraham, Isaac, and Israel, let it be known this day that You are Elohim in Israel, and I am Your servant; and that I have done all these things at Your word.
37 Hear me, Yahweh! Hear me, that this people may know that You are Yahweh Elohim; and that You have turned their hearts back to You again."

Yahweh answered by fire when Eliyahu called on His true name.

Melachim Aleph (1 Kings) 18:38-40
38 Then the fire of Yahweh fell and consumed the burnt sacrifice, and the wood, and the stones, and the dust: and it licked up the water that was in the trench.
39 Now when all the people saw it, they fell on their faces; and they said, "Yahweh! He is Elohim! Yahweh! He is Elohim!"
40 And Eliyahu said to them, "Seize the prophets of the Lord! Do not let one of them escape!" So they seized them, and Eliyahu brought them down to the Brook Kishon, and executed them there.

The first three commandments all deal with idolatry. In the first two, Yahweh says not to worship anyone other than Him, and not to make any graven images of Him. In the third He says not to let His name lie in ruins. We can make excuses for letting His name lie in ruins if we want, but Yahweh will not hold us guiltless, if we do that.

Shemote (Exodus) 20:7
7 "You shall not take the name of Yahweh your Elohim in vain, for Yahweh will not hold him guiltless who takes His name in vain."

If you love your spouse, are you sure to call your spouse by their correct name? This is all a simple part of love—calling our Husband by His name.

In Hosea 2:17 (2:19 in Hebrew), Yahweh says the day will come (after Armageddon) when He will take away the name of the Ba'als from Ephraim's mouth, and they (Ba'als) shall be remembered by their names no more.

This can only be the name *Lord* because that is the only name that the Ephraimites call on. No other name fits.

Hosea 2:17	
Hosea 2:17 17 For I will take from her mouth the names of the Baals, And they shall be remembered by their name no more.	(19) וַהֲסִרֹתִי אֶת שְׁמוֹת הַבְּעָלִים מִפִּיהָ ׀ וְלֹא יִזָּכְרוּ עוֹד בִּשְׁמָם

When we are reading Scripture, we are reading about spirits. We need to realize that Yahweh and the Lord are two separate deities. The *Lord* wants us to worship him on Sunday, Christmas, and Ishtar/Easter. He has a son named *Jesus* who came to do away with the bridal covenant (the Torah), as well as the bride (Israel). He is not the same deity as Yahweh.

Hosea 13:1 says that our forefathers were mighty, and that when they spoke, there was trembling. However, when they began to worship the Lord (rather than Yahweh) they incurred guilt. They "died" spiritually (and were no longer counted as Ephraimites). This is the seriousness of the third commandment.

Hoshea (Hosea) 13:1
1 When Ephraim spoke, there was trembling. He was exalted in Israel; but he incurred guilt through the Lord, and he died.

Yahweh is patient, but even His great patience has limits. Our forefathers did not see the importance of doing things His way, and eventually the time came when Yahweh was finished (Gomer) with Ephraim. He would no longer have mercy (Lo Ruhamah), so we would no longer be His people (Lo Ammi).

Because our forefathers did not value the inheritance Yahweh had given them, Yahweh sent the King of Assyria to take them out of the land, and sow them into the earth like seed, and their descendants would not return home for some 2,730 years.

Israel is Swallowed Up

In the last chapter we saw how the Ephraimites fell into idolatry and called Yahweh *Bel/Ba'al* (Lord). We also saw how Yahweh said He would sow them into the earth like seed for their disobedience. This would be the first step in fulfilling the promises given to Avraham and Ya'akov (Jacob), such that every family, every nation, and every clan would be blessed with their genetics, and thus become heir to the promise of salvation.

In the eighth century BCE, Yahweh sent the kings of Assyria to make several military incursions into the land of Israel. Around 722 BCE, the Ephraimite capital city of Samaria fell. The Ephraimites were taken out of the land, and were resettled in the lands that now make up modern-day Syria and Iraq. This was the natural result of turning away from His covenant—that they would not believe in Yahweh, and that they would worship idols.

Melachim Bet (2 Kings) 17:6-16
6 In the ninth year of Hosea, the king of Assyria took Samaria [the capital of Ephraim] and carried Israel away to Assyria, and placed them in Halah and by the Habor, the River of Gozan, and in the cities of the Medes.
7 For so it was that the children of Israel had sinned against Yahweh their Elohim, who had brought them up out of the land of Egypt, from under the hand of Pharaoh king of Egypt; and they had feared other gods,
8 and had walked in the statutes of the nations whom Yahweh had cast out from before the

115

children of Israel, and of the kings of Israel, which they had made.

9 Also the children of Israel secretly did against Yahweh their Elohim things that were not right, and they built for themselves high places in all their cities, from watchtower to fortified city.

10 They set up for themselves sacred pillars and wooden images on every high hill, and under every green tree.

11 There they burned incense on all the high places, like the nations whom Yahweh had carried away before them; and they did wicked things to provoke Yahweh to anger,

12 for they served idols, of which Yahweh had said to them, "You shall not do this thing."

13 Yet Yahweh testified against Israel and against Judah, by all of His prophets, every seer, saying, "Turn from your evil ways, and keep My commandments and My statutes, according to all the Torah which I commanded your fathers, and which I sent to you by My servants the prophets."

14 Nevertheless they would not hear, but stiffened their necks, like the necks of their fathers, who did not believe in Yahweh their Elohim [i.e., they did not obey Him].

15 And they rejected His statutes and His covenant that He had made with their fathers, and His testimonies which He had testified against them; they followed idols, became idolaters, and went after the nations who were all around them, concerning whom Yahweh had charged them that they should not do like them.

16 So they left all the commandments of Yahweh their Elohim, made for themselves a molded image and two calves, made a wooden image and worshiped all the host of heaven, and served The Lord [Bel/Ba'al].

We need to differentiate between the terms *dispersion* and *exile*, in order to keep things clear. In short, the term *dispersion* applies to the northern kingdom of Ephraim, while the term *exile* refers to the southern kingdom of Judah. When the ten tribes were taken to Assyria, this was called the *Assyrian Dispersion*, also called the *Diaspora* (the seeding). Sometimes it is called the Assyrian *Exile*, but the term *exile* technically applies to the two Jewish exiles.

1. The Assyrian Diaspora (Ephraim, 722 BCE)
2. The Babylonian Exile (Judah, 576 BCE)
3. The Roman Exile (Judah, 70 CE)

When the Assyrians conquered a new territory, they did not want any trouble with uprisings, so they took out anyone who had reason to see the old order restored. Their policy was to remove all but the poorest people out of the land, and resettle it with other ethnic groups from the surrounding territories. The idea was not only to cut the people's ties to the land, but also to destroy everyone's prior ethnic and religious identities through intermarriage.

Melachim Bet (2 Kings) 17:24
24 Then the king of Assyria brought people from Babylon, Cuthah, Ava, Hamath, and from Sepharvaim, and placed them in the cities of Samaria instead of the children of Israel; and they took possession of Samaria and dwelt in its cities.

The capital of the northern kingdom of Ephraim was in the mountains of Samaria—and when the Assyrians were finished taking away most of the Israelites, and bringing in the people of other nations, the result was a new mixed race called the *Samaritans*.

Yahweh hates idol worship, and the idolatrous religions of the Samaritans displeased Yahweh so much that He sent lions to attack them. Realizing that "the Elohim of the land" was not happy, the King of Assyria had one of the Ephraimite priests sent back to Samaria to teach the people how to keep the "rituals" of the land, not realizing that the northern kingdom had been practicing false worship ever since Jeroboam.

> Melachim Bet (2 Kings) 17:25-29
> 25 And it was so, at the beginning of their dwelling there, that they did not fear Yahweh; therefore Yahweh sent lions among them, which killed some of them.
> 26 So they spoke to the king of Assyria, saying, "The nations whom you have removed and placed in the cities of Samaria do not know the rituals of the Elohim of the land; therefore He has sent lions among them, and indeed, they are killing them because they do not know the rituals of the Elohim of the land."
> 27 Then the king of Assyria commanded, saying, "Send there one of the priests whom you brought from there; let him go and dwell there, and let him teach them the rituals of the Elohim of the land."
> 28 Then one of the priests whom they had carried away from Samaria came and dwelt in Bethel, and taught them how they should fear Yahweh.
> 29 However every nation continued to make elohim of its own, and put them in the shrines on the high places which the Samaritans had made, every nation in the cities where they dwelt.

Even though this unnamed priest was able to teach the Samaritans to fear Yahweh, verse 29 tells us that every nation (i.e., every religious group) continued to make idols of their own, and they put them in the shrines on the high places. So, just like the Christians would do many years later, they were fearing Yahweh, but were still serving their own mighty ones.

> Melachim Bet (2 Kings) 17:33-34
> 33 They [Samaritans] feared Yahweh; but they were serving their own mighty ones, according to the ruling of the nations to whom they had been exiled.
> 34 To this day they are doing according to the former rulings: They are not [truly] fearing Yahweh, nor do they [really] follow their laws or their right-rulings, which Yahweh had commanded the children of Ya'akov, whose name He made Israel,

Since the Samaritans kept a corrupt version of the Torah, the Jews avoided them—and there was enmity, suspicion and hostility between the Jews and the Samaritans. Meanwhile, the Ephraimites who had been scattered in Assyria were encouraged to assimilate and adopt the religious customs of the lands into which they were sown. They assimilated so well that they forgot all about Yahweh and His Torah. This took place in order to fulfill Hosea 8:8.

> Hoshea (Hosea) 8:8
> 8 "Israel is swallowed up;
> Now they are among the Gentiles
> Like a vessel in which is no pleasure."

Our Jewish brethren watched this from afar, and they recorded their impressions in an important historical document called the *Talmud*. Although the Talmud is not Scripture, it does record the innermost thoughts and reflections of the most respected Jewish religious authorities of those times. That is why it is so significant that in Talmud Tractate Yebamot 17A, the Jewish Sages record that the dispersed Ephraimites began to father "strange children." They called them "strange" because they no longer kept the Torah or spoke Hebrew, but had become "perfect heathens."

> When I mentioned the matter in the presence of Samuel he said to me, they [the Ephraimites] did not move from there until they [the Jewish sages] had declared them [Ephraimites] to be perfect heathens; as it is said in the Scriptures, They have dealt treacherously against the Lord, for they have begotten strange children.
> [Talmud Tractate Yebamot 17A, Soncino]

Now to make things even more interesting, there are two different words for *gentile* in Hebrew. One is *goy*, which refers to someone who has no relationship to the nation of Israel. The other is *ger*, which refers to someone who has had a relationship with Israel in the past, but who is not now part of the nation. Exactly how these words are applied depends on who is using them, and what his agenda is. Because Kepha (Peter) knew that the Ephraimites had been scattered to the four winds in order to fulfill the promises given to Avraham and Ya'akov, he writes his epistle to the strangers of the (Assyrian) Dispersion (i.e., to the Ephraimites).

> Kepha Aleph (1 Peter) 1:1
> 1 Kepha, an apostle of Yeshua Messiah, to the pilgrims of the [Assyrian] Dispersion in Pontus, Galatia, Cappadocia, Asia, and Bithynia....

Kepha knew that the Ephraimites were strangers (gerim, plural of *ger*) because the prophecies in Hosea and elsewhere said they would someday come back. The Jewish sages who wrote the Talmud surely knew this also, or they would not have been tracking the movements of the Ephraimites. Yet, rather than call the Ephraimites *gerim* (strangers), the sages called the Ephraimites "perfect heathens," meaning they were indistinguishable from the *goyim* (plural of *goy*).

In Talmud Tractate Yebamot 17A, the Jews ruled that the Ephraimites were to be thought of as goyim (no relation to Israel) from that time forward. This is one reason why so many of our Jewish brothers have such a hard time with the Two House Theory today: ethnicity is central to their belief set. They believe that there are *Jews* and there are *goyim*. They believe all twelve tribes must assimilate into the tribe of Judah—and they do not understand or appreciate any role that the rest of the tribes have to play, because it detracts from what they see as their preeminent lead role.

Even those Jews who *did* understand that the lost ten tribes had to be scattered, and would be regathered, had no idea how the lost ten tribes could be regathered to the nation when their genealogies were rapidly disappearing. The definition of a *messiah* is that of a divinely-anointed leader who brings the lost and scattered of Israel back to the land, and to the eternal covenant—but how, the Jews must have wondered, could anyone ever bring the Ephraimites back after they had become so thoroughly assimilated, and could no longer be identified genealogically?

Fulfilling the Prophecies

In the last chapter we saw how the lost ten tribes of Israel were sent into the dispersion for disobedience. But how long were they to be gone? When were they to return? Several of the prophecies give us answers to these questions, and more.

Ezekiel was told to lie on his left side for 390 days. Each day was symbolic of a year that Ephraim was to remain in the dispersion (outside the land).

> Yehezqel (Ezekiel) 4:4-5
> 4 "Lie also on your left side, and lay the iniquity of the house of Israel upon it. According to the number of the days that you lie on it, you shall bear their iniquity.
> 5 For I have laid on you the years of their iniquity, according to the number of the days: three hundred and ninety days; so you shall bear the iniquity of the house of Israel [Ephraim]."

If the lost tribes would repent after the 390 years, they would come home; but Leviticus tells us that those who do not repent at the end of being punished will have their time of punishment multiplied sevenfold.

> Vayiqra (Leviticus) 26:14-18
> 14 "'But if you do not obey Me, and do not observe all these commandments,
> 15 and if you despise My statutes, or if your soul abhors My judgments, so that you do not perform all My commandments, but break My covenant,
> 16 I also will do this to you: I will even appoint terror over you, wasting disease and fever which

shall consume the eyes and cause sorrow of heart. And you shall sow your seed in vain, for your enemies shall eat it.

17 I will set My face against you, and you shall be defeated by your enemies. Those who hate you shall reign over you, and you shall flee when no one pursues you.

18 'And after all this, if you [still] do not obey Me, then I will punish you seven times more for your sins.'"

The Assyrians did not carry the Ephraimites out of the land all at once. Rather, they began invading around 734 BCE, and then the campaigns went on for many years. If we use 734 as a start point, and add 390 years to that, we arrive at 344 BCE. Clearly, Ephraim did not repent then, so Yahweh multiplied her punishment seven times, for a total of 2,730 years.

If Ephraim's punishment began in 734 BCE, then 2,730 years later brings us to 1996 CE. If this calculation is correct, then the Ephraimite nation would start to be restored about then; and that is what happened. While the Ephraimite movement had started some decades earlier, it began to flourish and grow around 1996 CE, as Yahweh began to turn back Ephraim's punishment.

Scripture gives us several other major witnesses to the restoration of the house of Ephraim. One of these witnesses is in the book of Hosea. Hosea was a prophet to the northern kingdom of Ephraim. He was speaking about the Ephraimites when he prophesied:

Hoshea (Hosea) 6:2
2 "After two days He will revive us;
On the third day He will raise us up,
That we may live in His sight."

Kepha (Peter) tells us not to forget that a prophetic day with Yahweh is equal to a thousand earth years.

Kepha Bet (2 Peter) 3:8
8 But, beloved, do not forget this one thing, that with Yahweh, one day is as a thousand years, and a thousand years as one day.

If a prophetic day is as a thousand years, then the two prophetic days of Hosea 6:2 represent two thousand earth years. Therefore, what Hosea says is that after two thousand years, the Ephraimites will be raised up, so that they might again live in Yahweh's favor (sight).

The phrase "the third day" gives us a *remez* (hint) that this prophecy relates to Yeshua, since He was raised on the third day.

Marqaus (Mark) 9:31
31 "And after He is killed, He will rise the third day."

Modern scholarship tells us that the Messiah was born about 4 BCE. If we add two thousand years to 4 BCE, we come to about 1996 CE, which is the same year Ezekiel 4 says Ephraim's punishment ran out (above). This means we are now in the third prophetic day, which is why we are beginning to see the house of Israel restored all around the world.

Because Avraham obeyed Yahweh's voice, and was willing to sacrifice his only son, Yahweh said that all of the families of the earth would be blessed in him. It is important that we see this particular passage only refers to Avraham's physical offspring.

B'reisheet (Genesis) 17:4-8

4 "As for Me, behold, My covenant is with you, and you shall be a father of many nations.

5 No longer shall your name be called Avram, but your name shall be Avraham; for I have made you a father of many nations.

6 I will make you exceedingly fruitful; and I will make nations of you, and kings shall come from you.

7 And I will establish My covenant between Me and you and your descendants after you in their generations, for an everlasting covenant, to be Elohim to you and your descendants after you.

8 Also I give to you and your descendants after you the land in which you are a stranger, all the land of Canaan, as an everlasting possession; and I will be their Elohim."

Avraham's children would become like the stars of the heavens, and like the sand of the seashore, which is neither numbered nor counted—because Avraham had obeyed Yahweh's voice.

B'reisheet (Genesis) 22:15-18

15 Then the messenger of Yahweh called to Avraham a second time out of heaven,

16 and said: "By Myself I have sworn, says Yahweh, because you have done this thing, and have not withheld your son, your only son —

17 blessing I will bless you, and multiplying I will multiply your descendants as the stars of the heaven and as the sand which is on the seashore; and your descendants shall possess the gate of their enemies.

18 In your seed all the nations of the earth shall be blessed, because you have obeyed My voice."

The above blessings speak of physical multiplicity, but there was also a spiritual blessing of salvation, so that the divine relationship that was lost in the Garden of Eden could be restored. Yeshua tells us that salvation is of the Jews (John 4:22), but the roots of this promise are given in Genesis 17, where Elohim said that the covenant of redemption and salvation in Yeshua would not come through Ishmael, but through Yitzhak (Isaac).

B'reisheet (Genesis) 17:19-21
19 Then Elohim said: "No, Sarah your wife shall bear you a son, and you shall call his name Yitzhak; I will establish My covenant with him for an everlasting covenant, and with his descendants after him.
20 And as for Ishmael, I have heard you. Behold, I have blessed him, and will make him fruitful, and will multiply him exceedingly. He shall beget twelve princes, and I will make him a great nation.
21 But My covenant I will establish with Yitzhak, whom Sarah shall bear to you at this set time next year."

If we look closely, in Genesis 28:14 (below) we will see that there were two blessings given to Ya'akov (Jacob)/Israel. One would be genetic (referring to Israel's physical descendants), while the other referred to Ya'akov's seed (meaning Yeshua, and the spiritual salvation that would come through Him).

B'reisheet (Genesis) 28:10-15
10 Now Ya'akov went out from Beersheba and went toward Haran.
11 So he came to a certain place and stayed there all night, because the sun had set. And he took one of the stones of that place and put it at his head, and he lay down in that place to sleep.

127

12 Then he dreamed, and behold, a ladder was set up on the earth, and its top reached to heaven; and there the angels of Elohim were ascending and descending on it.

13 And behold, Yahweh stood above it and said: "I am Yahweh Elohim of Avraham your father and the Elohim of Yitzhak; the land on which you lie I will give to you and your descendants.

14 Also your descendants shall be as the dust of the earth; you shall spread abroad to the west and the east, to the north and the south; and in you [genetically] and in your seed [Yeshua] all the families of the earth shall be blessed.

15 Behold, I am with you and will keep you wherever you go, and will bring you back to this land; for I will not leave you until I have done what I have spoken to you."

Some people have a hard time believing that Avraham's genetics could spread to every continent in the world, and become part of every nation, every tribe, every clan, and every family over the course of four thousand years or so. But why should we doubt it? Israelites have always been a commerce-and-trade-loving people, and they have always gone wherever there is money to be found. Ancient trade routes went south into Africa, and east into India and China, and archaeology shows us that the ancient Israelites also traveled to the Americas. So if the Israelites were in Africa, Asia, the Americas, and Europe, then why should we be surprised that Avraham's genetics would make their way into every nation, every clan, and every family over a four thousand year period?

If we pour chlorine into one end of a swimming pool, eventually it makes its way all through the pool. Now let us consider that Israelite genetics were infused into mankind's gene pool wherever there were trade routes, over land and by sea. How hard is it to permeate the world's gene pool when you lace it with Israelite genetics over many different routes, over millennia?

Hypothetically, even if a man somewhere on earth (for example, in the Amazon jungle) did not have any of Avraham's genetics, he could still graft into the nation of Israel by faith. Genetics would not be an issue. In fact, the idea of grafting into the nation by faith long predates Yeshua. For example, Rahab joined the nation although she was a Canaanite (Joshua 6), and Ruth the Moabitess went on to become King David's great-grandmother. She became an Israelite the moment she gave her allegiance to Yahweh.

> Root (Ruth) 1:16
> 16 But Root said: "Entreat me not to leave you, Or to turn back from following after you; For wherever you go, I will go; And wherever you lodge, I will lodge; Your people shall be my people, And your Elohim, my Elohim."

While Yahweh has used certain genetic groups of people to fulfill His purposes, ultimately Scripture is not a book about genetics—Scripture is a book about giving our allegiance and obedience to Yahweh, and becoming the best bride we can for Him. Genetics only show us the historical means by which Yahweh chooses to fulfill His prophecies.

The ten tribes went into the dispersion despite their genes. Brokenness and obedience would have served them much better. Still, it helps to understand the mechanics of what took place historically. Jacob's dream, recorded in Genesis 28, helps us understand prophecies that could only be fulfilled by the dispersing of the tribes. Let us read it closely, for there are some things which both Jewish and Christian scholars often miss.

B'reisheet (Genesis) 28:10-15
10 And Ya'akov went out from Be'er-Sheva and went toward Haran.
11 And he came on a place and stayed the night there, for the sun had gone. And he took stones of the place and placed them at his head; and he lay down in that place.
12 And he dreamed; and behold! A ladder was set up on the earth, its top reaching toward the heavens. And behold! The angels of Elohim were going up and down on it!
13 And behold! Yahweh stood above it and said, "I am Yahweh, the Elohim of your father Avraham, and the Elohim of Isaac. The land on which you are lying, I give it to you [genetically], and to your seed.
14 And your seed shall be as the dust of the earth, and you [Israel's children] shall spread to the west, and to the east, and to the north and to the south; and all the families of the earth shall be blessed in you [genetically]; and [in] your Seed [Yeshua].
15 And behold! I will be with you and will guard you in every place in which you may go, and will bring you back to this land. For I will not forsake you until I have surely done all that I have spoken to you."

In Galatians 3:16, the Apostle Shaul (Paul) tells us that this word "seed" is singular, and refers to Yeshua.

Galatim (Galatians) 3:16

16 Now to Abraham and his Seed were the promises made. He does not say, "And to seeds", as of many, but as of one, "And to your Seed", who is the Messiah.

There are two blessings in Genesis 28:14 (above). In addition to being blessed in Yeshua, all the families of the earth would be blessed in Ya'akov, and could now receive salvation in Yeshua, because they would have Ya'akov's righteous genetics. Of course, they still need to accept Yeshua, and be filled with His Spirit; yet because Christianity does not understand the genetic component, they only understand grafting in by faith. Sadly, this yields a lopsided picture.

> Galatim (Galatians) 3:26-29
> 26 For you are all sons of Elohim through faith in Messiah Yeshua.
> 27 For as many of you as were immersed into Messiah have put on Messiah.
> 28 There is neither Jew nor Greek [Hellenized Jew], there is neither slave nor free, there is neither male nor female; for you are all one in Messiah Yeshua.
> 29 And if you are Messiah's, then you are Abraham's seed, and heirs according to the promise.

The Christians understand that if we are grafted in by favor through faith in Messiah Yeshua, then we are heirs to the promise of salvation—but they don't understand the need for a literal genetic component. Yet, if there is no genetic component, then there is no way for Yahweh to fulfill the promise He gave to Israel in Genesis 28:13-15, that He would scatter his descendants to the four winds, bless all the families of the earth in his genetics, and then later bring a remnant of their descendants back to the land of Israel.

B'reisheet (Genesis) 28:13-15
13 And behold! Yahweh stood above it and said, "I am Yahweh, the Elohim of your father Avraham, and the Elohim of Isaac. The land on which you are lying, I give it to you [genetically], and to your seed.
14 And your seed shall be as the dust of the earth, and you [Israel's children] shall spread to the west, and to the east, and to the north and to the south; and all the families of the earth shall be blessed in you [genetically]; and [in] your seed [Yeshua].
15 And behold! I will be with you and will guard you in every place in which you may go, and will bring you back to this land. For I will not forsake you until I have surely done all that I have spoken to you."

Then, in Genesis 35:10-12, we are told that Israel would father "a nation" (Judah) and a "company of nations" (the Christian nations of Europe).

B'reisheet (Genesis) 35:10-12
10 And Elohim said to him, "Your name is Ya'akov; your name shall not be called Ya'akov anymore, but Israel shall be your name." So He called his name Israel.
11 Also Elohim said to him: "I am Elohim Almighty. Be fruitful and multiply; a [Jewish] nation and a company of [Christian] nations shall proceed from you, and kings shall come from your body.

132

12 The land which I gave Abraham and Isaac I give to you; and to your descendants after you I give this land."

Some people argue that the Jews of today are not really Jewish, since many of them descend from white European stock. However, as we saw earlier, when someone joins himself to the nation of Israel, and gives allegiance to Yahweh, he becomes an Israelite. This principle extends to the Jewish nation, as well as to the Ephraimites. If someone joins himself to the Jewish nation and sojourns as a Jew, he becomes Jewish, no matter what his ethnicity used to be.

Astonishingly, some people claim verse 11 refers to Ishmael (the Muslim people). However, this cannot be, in that we are told that the "company of nations" would descend from Ya'akov, whereas the Muslim people descend from Ishmael. Yet various prophecies tell us that after some great wars in the Middle East, many of the Muslim people will also convert to the worship of Yahweh.

Yeshayahu (Isaiah) 19:23-25
23 In that day there will be a highway from Egypt to Assyria, and the Assyrian will come into Egypt and the Egyptian into Assyria, and the Egyptians will serve with the Assyrians.
24 In that day Israel will be one of three with Egypt and Assyria — a blessing in the midst of the land,
25 whom Yahweh of hosts shall bless, saying, "Blessed is Egypt My people, and Assyria the work of My hands, and Israel My inheritance."

Judah and Ephraim are now scattered to the corners of the earth. They are mixed with every tribe and tongue and people. Every nation, every clan, and every family is blessed with Israel's genetics, and is capable of receiving Yeshua.

The Two Houses in the New Covenant

We spoke earlier about of the Assyrian Dispersion, and how Yahweh sent the Assyrians to take Ephraim away, but the Assyrians were not particular. They also took away some of the people from the southern tribes (Judah and Benjamin). This may be why Ya'akov (James) writes his epistle not just to the ten tribes of the dispersion, but to the twelve.

James 1:1	BGT **James 1:1** Ἰάκωβος
1 "Ya'akov (James), a servant of Elohim and of the Master Yeshua Messiah, to the twelve tribes who are in the diaspora: Greetings."	θεοῦ καὶ κυρίου Ἰησοῦ Χριστοῦ δοῦλος ταῖς δώδεκα φυλαῖς ταῖς ἐν τῇ διασπορᾷ χαίρειν.

While the term *dispersion* (διασπορᾷ) normally refers to the ten northern tribes, it is also correct that Ya'akov addresses the twelve tribes. However, what we need to see is that he is not addressing non-Israelite Christians, but the twelve tribes of Israel.

The Apostle Kepha (Peter) also addresses those of the dispersion, calling them "strangers" (παρεπιδήμοις).

1 Peter 1:1	BGT **1 Peter 1:1** Πέτρος
1 "Kepha, an emissary of Yeshua Messiah to the Chosen: strangers of the	ἀπόστολος Ἰησοῦ Χριστοῦ ἐκλεκτοῖς παρεπιδήμοις διασπορᾶς

Dispersion in Pontos, Galatia, Kappadokia, Asia, and Bithunia;"	Πόντου, Γαλατίας, Καππαδοκίας, Ἀσίας καὶ Βιθυνίας, (1Pe 1:1 BGT)

As stated previously in this book, there are two words for *gentile* in Hebrew. A *ger* is someone who used to be part of the nation of Israel, but who has drifted away and is now estranged. In contrast, a *goy* is a gentile who has no relationship with the nation of Israel. While you deal kindly with *goyim* (plural of *goy)*, you keep them out of your assembly.

The Christian church tells us that Kepha is addressing the goyim, because the church believes Yeshua came to do away with Israel and replace them with the goyim. However, that does not fit the context. It makes more sense that Kepha is writing to *gerim* (plural of *ger)*, because he calls them "an elect race" and "a set apart nation" (which is something that goyim can never be). He also quotes Hosea, telling them they are the lost ten tribes of Ephraim being called back into the covenant.

> Kepha Aleph (1 Peter) 2:9-10
> 9 But you are an elect race, a royal priesthood, a set apart nation, a people for a possession, so that you may openly speak of the virtues of the One who has called you out of darkness, into His marvelous light.
> 10 You who were then not a people (Lo-Ammi), but now are the "people of Elohim"; the one not pitied then (Lo-Ruhamah), but now pitied (Ruhamah).

This is a clear, direct reference to Hosea 1:8-10, which we saw earlier.

Hoshea (Hosea) 1:8-10
8 Now when she had weaned Lo-Ruhamah, she conceived and bore a son.
9 Then Elohim said: "Call his name Lo-Ammi, for you are not My people, and I will not be your Elohim.
10 Yet the number of the children of Israel Shall be as the sand of the sea, Which cannot be measured or numbered. And it shall come to pass In the place where it was said to them, 'You are not My people,' There it shall be said to them, 'You are sons of the living Elohim."

Shaul (Paul) also quotes Hosea to show the gerim that they are actually returning Ephraimites.

Romim (Romans) 9:24-26
24 … even us whom He called, not of the Jews only, but also of the Gentiles [Ephraim]?
25 As He says also in Hosea: "I will call them My people [Ammi] who were not My people [Lo Ammi], And her beloved [Ruhamah], who was not beloved [Lo Ruhamah]."
26 "And it shall come to pass in the place where it was said to them, ' You are not My people,' There they shall be called sons of the living Elohim."

Kepha and Shaul are saying that the ten lost tribes are being called back to rejoin the nation of Israel, so that there will be twelve tribes again.

In complete contrast, the church teaches what is known as *replacement theology*, which is that the church replaced (or did away with) the Jews. Shaul tells the Ephraimites clearly that Yahweh has not cast away their Jewish brethren.

Romim (Romans) 11:1-2
1 I say then, has Elohim cast away His people [forever]? Elohim forbid; for I also am an Israelite, of the seed of Abraham, of the tribe of Benjamin.
2 Elohim has not cast away His people whom He foreknew.

Remembering that Yahweh works in patterns, we recognize the same pattern from the time of Jeroboam, when Israel was to become the new lead house (provided they obeyed Yahweh's Torah). The Jews were to be afflicted (but not forever).

Melachim Aleph (1 Kings) 11:39
39 And I will afflict the descendants of David [the Jews] because of this, but not forever.

Shaul also tried to make it clear that this affliction would not be permanent, but only for a time (and a purpose).

Romim (Romans) 11:11
11 I say then, have they stumbled that they should fall? Certainly not!

Shaul says Judah will also accept Yeshua, as soon as Ephraim has fulfilled the Great Commission and spread the true Good News to the ends of the earth, and the fullness of the gentiles has come in.

Romim (Romans) 11:25-27
25 For I do not desire, brethren, that you should be ignorant of this secret, lest you should be wise in your own estimation: that blindness in part has happened to Israel [meaning both Houses here] until the fullness of the Gentiles [Ephraim] has come in.

26 And so all Israel [both houses] shall be saved, as it is written: "The Deliverer will come out of Zion, And He will turn away iniquity from Jacob [quoting Isaiah 59:20];
27 "For this is My covenant with them, When I take away their sins [quoting Isaiah 27:9]."

Sometimes Ephraimites think that they have all of the truth, while Judah has none. This is a mistake. As we will see, both houses were to be partially blinded for a time, and for a purpose. Ephraim would know Yeshua, but reject the Torah. This is so the Christians could take their torahless version of the Good News to the ends of the earth. Judah, conversely, would be blind to Yeshua because his job was to preserve an inheritance for Ephraim to come home to. However, Shaul tells us Judah will ultimately come to know Yeshua, because the Jews' election as children of the covenant is irrevocable.

Romim (Romans) 11:28-29
28 Concerning the Good News they are enemies for your sake, but concerning the election they are beloved for the sake of the fathers;
29 for the gifts and the calling of Elohim are irrevocable.

Neither torahless Christianity nor Yeshualess Judaism is sufficient. Ephraim is like a woman who insists she loves her husband, but does not want to do what He asks. Conversely, Judah does much of what Yeshua asks, but she uses her partial obedience as an excuse to lock Him out of her house. Curiously, both of these expect to be taken in marriage. However, until they believe on Him, obey His commandments in His Spirit of love, and continuously submit to His Spirit, their worship of Him is far from complete.

139

More than a hundred years after the lost ten tribes were taken away in the Assyrian Diaspora, the Jews of the southern kingdom were carried away in an exile of their own. This second Jewish exile, known as the *Babylonian Exile*, lasted approximately seventy years. At the end of that time, roughly 10 percent of the Jews came back to the land (in the days of Ezra and Nehemiah). The other 90 percent remained out in Babylon where living conditions were easier. Like the Ephraimites, they intermarried and assimilated into the culture. Then, as a result of military conquest, trade, and other factors, Judah's seed also spread to the four winds in fulfillment of the prophecies given to Avraham and Ya'akov. Because of this, Kepha poetically likens their calling to that of their Ephraimite brothers.

Kepha Aleph (1 Peter) 5:13
13 She who is in Babylon [the 90% of Judah still out in the Babylonian Exile], chosen together with you [the lost ten tribes still in the diaspora] greets you: also my son [disciple], Mark.

Symbolism and poetry is common in Jewish literature, and Kepha is not alone in using it. John uses Leah and Rachel as symbols of their respective houses (Judah and Joseph/Ephraim). He says that all those (Jews) who have known the truth love their Ephraimite brothers.

Yochanan Bet (2 John) 1:1
1 The elder [brother, meaning the house of Judah], to a chosen lady [Rachel] and her children [meaning the house of Joseph/Ephraim], whom I love in truth; and not only I, but also those who have known the truth.

John was of the house of Judah, and Judah was born to Leah. He tells the Ephraimites that the children (the Jews) of their chosen sister (Leah) greet them.

Yochanan Bet (2 John) 1:13
13 The children [meaning the house of Judah] of your chosen sister [Leah] greet you: Amein.

Yeshua speaks of the return of the Ephraimites in the parable of the prodigal son. The church teaches this parable is nothing more than a beautiful story about a backslidden sinner who repents of his sin. However, remembering that the name Ephraim literally means *prodigious,* and that Judah is older than Ephraim, let us understand this parable as a prophetic picture of the return of the lost ten tribes.

Luqa (Luke) 15:11-19
11 And Yeshua said, "A certain Man (Yahweh) had two sons. And the younger of them [Ephraim] said to the Father, 'Father, give me that part of the goods falling to me;' and He divided the inheritance between them.
13 "And not too many days after, gathering up all things, the younger son [Ephraim] went away to a distant country [in the Assyrian Dispersion]; and there he wasted his goods [the law and the language], living dissolutely [and becoming a "perfect heathen"].
14 "But having lost all his goods, a severe famine [a famine of spiritual food, prophesied in Amos 8:11] came through that country; and he began to be in need. And going, he was joined to one of the citizens of that country [the pope]; and he sent him into his fields, to feed the pigs [idols]. And he longed to fill his stomach with the pods that the

pigs ate; but no one gave him anything [that would sustain him spiritually].

17 "But coming to himself [in the Protestant Reformation], he said 'How many of my Father's servants have plenty of loaves [bread is symbolic of the Torah]; but I am perishing with famine!

18 'Rising up, I will go to my Father and I will say to Him, "Father, I have sinned against the Heaven and against you, and am no longer worthy to be called Your son.

19 Make me as one of your hired servants!"'"

As we mentioned earlier, while the lost ten tribes did disperse in all four directions, the bulk of them migrated north and west with the rise and the fall of empires. Eventually their migrations end in what would later become Protestant Northwestern Europe. After the Catholics had dominated Europe for some 1,260 years, the children of Ephraim would break away from the pope (i.e., the little horn), and they would begin seeking Yahweh's face more directly. As a result, Yahweh blessed them with more prosperity and technological achievement than had ever before been known.

Luqa (Luke) 15:20-24

20 "And rising up [in the Protestant Reformation] he came to his Father; but he yet being far away [from the original Nazarene faith] his Father saw him, and was moved with pity; and running, He fell on his neck and fervently kissed him [though he was still as yet only a Protestant Christian].

21 "And the son [Ephraim] said to Him, 'Father, I have sinned against Heaven, and before You, and no longer am worthy to be called Your son.'

22 "But the Father said to His slaves, 'Bring out the best robe and clothe him [literally, Joseph's

142

coat], and give a ring for his hand [Joseph's signet], and sandals for his feet!
23 And bring the fattened calf, and slaughter it! And let us eat and be merry;
24 for this son [Ephraim] of Mine was dead, and is alive again; and was lost, and is found!' And they began to be merry."

In the parable, when the Father saw Ephraim a long way off, ran to him, fell on his neck, and kissed him, this is symbolic of how Yahweh blessed the Protestant nations beyond all others, simply for seeking His face. This is a source of resentment for Judah, who has kept the Torah for millennia without ever having received the same kinds of blessings of safety and easy prosperity that the Protestant people have enjoyed.

Luqa (Luke) 15:25-28
25 "But his older son [Judah] was in the field; and coming, as he drew near to the house [temple] he heard music and dances.
26 "And having called one of the children to him, [Judah] inquired as to what this might be;
27 and he said to him, 'Your brother [Ephraim] came, and your Father killed the fattened calf, because he received him back in health.'
28 "But he [Judah] was enraged, and did not desire to go in. Then coming out, his Father begged him."

Judah is indignant that Ephraim could despise his inheritance (much like Esau despised it), and still be welcomed back home.

Luqa (Luke) 15:29-31
29 "But answering, he [Judah] said to the Father, 'Behold, how many years have I served you, and

never did I transgress a commandment of yours! But you never gave me a young goat, so that I might rejoice with my friends!

30 But when this son of yours came [he does not even call Ephraim his brother], the one having devoured your livelihood with harlots [idols, icons, false religious traditions, false festival dates, false festival sites, etc.] you killed the fattened calf for him!'

31 "But He said to him, 'Child, you are always with me, and all of My things are yours. But to be merry and to rejoice was right! For this brother of yours was dead, and is alive again! And was lost, and is found.'"

Because the Jews put Yeshua to death, Christians can sometimes have difficulty understanding why Judah would be incredulous. However, Judah has kept a variation of the Torah for thousands of years, even though Ephraim persecuted him for it. Ephraim subjected Judah to repeated pogroms, inquisitions, crusades, and massacres. Judah is upset that Ephraim could walk away from the covenant, worship idols, and try to change the Torah, and yet the Father still orders His servants to clothe Ephraim in the best robe (i.e., Joseph's coat), give him a signet ring (Joseph's signet ring), and bring sandals for his feet (as only slaves went barefoot). In Judah's mind, this is a tremendous injustice.

Scripture tells us that the end is known from the beginning; thus the key to comprehending this turn of events is to understand the allusion to Joseph's coat. In Genesis, Judah sold Joseph into slavery; and Joseph later went to prison for a crime he never committed. This is symbolic of how Judah drove the Nazarenes out from the temple for believing on Yeshua (which is the

144

farthest thing from a crime). Thus it is right that Yahweh would welcome the prodigal son (i.e., Joseph/Ephraim) back home.

Joseph served Pharaoh honorably, and his Elohim-given abilities brought him great power and prestige. He was eventually able to use his position to save the lives of many people, including his father and brothers. For many years the Christians were thought to be the underlying power in America, and America's Christians have historically demanded that their leaders support the State of Israel (at least since 1948).

Joseph's separation from his family is significant as well. Separation (consecration) from one's own people is highly regarded in Scripture. Although Yahweh created man as a social being (Genesis 2:18), there are some circumstances in which men must be separated from their brothers (and even from normal life) in order to serve Yahweh better. In the language of Scripture, these individuals are thought to be set apart from the world. While this kind of separation leads to trials, it is associated with eternal blessing.

While the twelve tribes are in every country, scholars sometimes associate America with the prophetic tribe of Ephraim/Joseph. Many of the early American settlers came to escape religious persecution in Europe, and to seek freedom to follow Scripture as they saw fit. In a sense, they had to leave their former countries involuntarily, just as Joseph was sent into Egypt involuntarily. Similarly, the blessings Israel gave over Joseph speak of a land that resembles America.

B'reisheet (Genesis) 49:25-26
25 "By the Elohim of your father who will help you, and by the Almighty who will bless you with

blessings of heaven above, blessings of the deep that lies beneath, blessings of the breasts and of the womb.

26 The blessings of your father have excelled the blessings of my ancestors, up to the utmost bound of the everlasting hills.

These shall be on the head of Joseph, and on the crown of the head of him who was separated from his brothers."

Moshe (Moses) also gives Joseph a special blessing for having been separated from his brothers.

Devarim (Deuteronomy) 33:13-16

13 And of Joseph he said:

"Blessed of Yahweh is his land, with the precious things of heaven, with the dew, and the deep lying beneath,

14 With the precious fruits of the sun, with the precious produce of the months,

15 With the best things of the ancient mountains, with the precious things of the everlasting hills,

16 With the precious things of the earth and its fullness, and the favor of Him who dwelt in the bush. Let this blessing come upon the head of Joseph, and upon the crown of the head of him who was separated from his brothers."

Yahweh allowed Joseph to enter Egypt ahead of his brothers, so that life could be preserved by means of a great deliverance. In this, Joseph is a foreshadow of the Messiah.

B'reisheet (Genesis) 45:5, 7

5 "But now, do not therefore be grieved or angry with yourselves because you sold me here; for Elohim sent me before you to preserve life....

146

7 And Elohim sent me before you to preserve a posterity for you in the earth; and to save your lives by a great deliverance."

Earlier we saw that the apostles understood Ephraim's role in fulfilling prophecy. It is also clear that the apostles knew the two houses would someday be reunited, which is why they asked Yeshua if He was going to restore the kingdom to the house of Israel at that time.

Ma'asei (Acts) 1:6
6 Therefore, when they had come together, they asked Him [Yeshua], saying, "Master, will You at this time restore the kingdom to [the house of] Israel?"

The time to restore the literal kingdom to the house of Israel was not then at hand (nor is it at hand at the time of this writing in 2014). It was only time for Yeshua's disciples to begin forming an international spiritual kingdom. They would gather Joseph's lost children, who had been sent ahead of them to the four corners of the earth. The process was interrupted by the pope (who built an alternate spiritual kingdom worldwide), but once Ephraim's captivity was over, the Spirit began bringing a remnant of Ephraim's lost and wayward prodigal sons back to the covenant, generation by generation, by the Spirit of Yeshua, the great Deliverer.

Yeshua Rebukes the Rabbis

When the Prophet Eliyahu (Elijah) fled from Ahab and Jezebel, he went to dwell at Mount Sinai (which is Horeb). While he was there, "a voice came to him" from Yahweh.

Melachim Aleph (1 Kings) 19:11-13
11 Then He said, "Go out, and stand on the mountain before Yahweh." And behold, Yahweh passed by, and a great and strong wind tore into the mountains and broke the rocks in pieces before Yahweh, but Yahweh was not in the wind; and after the wind an earthquake, but Yahweh was not in the earthquake;
12 and after the earthquake a fire, but Yahweh was not in the fire; and after the fire a still small voice.
13 So it was, when Eliyahu heard it, that he wrapped his face in his mantle and went out and stood in the entrance of the cave. Suddenly a voice came to him, and said, "What are you doing here, Eliyahu?"

While Yahweh can speak in an audible voice, usually He speaks in a still small voice. People experience this still small voice in different ways, but the point is that He wants us to listen for it continuously, and obey it, for this is how He guides the steps of the wise.

Yeshayahu (Isaiah) 30:21
21 "Your ears shall hear a word behind you, saying, 'This is the way, walk in it,' Whenever you turn to the right hand Or whenever you turn to the left."

Yahweh is clear that not only are we to obey His written commandments, He also wants us to obey His voice.

Devarim (Deuteronomy) 13:4
4 You shall walk after Yahweh your Elohim and fear Him, and keep His commandments and obey His voice; you shall serve Him and hold fast to Him.

Yahweh tells us that if we will both obey His voice and keep His covenant (Torah), then we will be a special treasure to Him above all peoples. Isn't that what we want?

Shemote (Exodus) 19:5
5 "Now therefore, if you will indeed obey My voice and keep My covenant [Torah], then you shall be a special treasure to Me above all people; for all the earth is Mine."

Yahweh is a loving Father, and He uses His voice to keep us from trouble. In the Garden of Eden, Yahweh told Adam and Havvah (Eve) not to eat of the tree of the knowledge of good and evil. However, the serpent told Havvah she could disobey Yahweh's voice, and still live. The serpent also implied that she would no longer need to hear or obey Yahweh's voice, because she herself would become like Elohim, knowing how to decide for herself what was good, and what was evil.

B'reisheet (Genesis) 3:4-5
4 Then the serpent said to the woman, "You will not surely die.
5 For Elohim knows that in the day you eat of it your eyes will be opened, and you will be like Elohim, knowing good and evil."

Satan tempted Havvah, suggesting that she would know what was best for her. However, she couldn't discern what was best; she just thought she could. Havvah became deceived—and, as we saw earlier, Havvah symbolizes Israel.

Havvah stopped listening for His voice—and since she stopped listening, she stopped obeying. Just as an earthly child would fall from his father's favor if he refused to listen to his father's voice, Havvah also fell from favor.

It is not enough for us just to know who Yahweh is; and it is not enough for us just to obey His written Torah. Yahweh wants a love relationship with us, such that we listen for His still small spiritual voice, and obey it. This will restore the broken communication that was lost in the Garden of Eden.

In earlier chapters we saw how the northern ten tribes of Ephraim had been sent into the Assyrian Dispersion for disobedience. Ephraim had been gone for over a hundred years when Jeremiah told the Jews that unless they got serious about hearing and obeying His voice, they also would go into exile.

Yirmeyahu (Jeremiah) 7:23-24
23 "But this is what I commanded them, saying, 'Obey My voice, and I will be your Elohim, and you shall be My people. And walk in all the ways that I have commanded you, that it may be well with you.'
24 Yet they did not obey or incline their ear, but followed the counsels and the dictates of their evil hearts, and went backward and not forward."

Judah would be in captivity in Babylon seventy years, after which time Yahweh would bring them home.

> Yirmeyahu (Jeremiah) 29:10
> 10 For thus says Yahweh: "After seventy years are completed at Babylon, I will visit you, and perform My good word toward you, and cause you to return to this place."

Over the next seventy years, however, the foundations of the Jewish faith would be subtly altered.

Just as the Assyrians relocated the people they had conquered, and encouraged them to assimilate, the Babylonians also scattered the peoples they had conquered, and encouraged them to assimilate. The Babylonians scattered those they conquered within their own borders, treated them well, and encouraged them to become Babylonian citizens. This strategy was very effective. When the people saw that they had a materially rich life in Babylon, not only did they not want to resist, but many of them lost their desire to go back to their former countries.

All of this led to a crisis of leadership within the Jewish nation. The Levitical order could not survive without a temple, because without a temple, the people had no place to bring their tithes and offerings—and without funding, the Levitical order soon collapsed. This left the Jewish people without spiritual leadership—and without spiritual leadership the people soon began to lose their sense of national identity, and they began assimilating into Babylon.

The Levitical priesthood had to form a new priesthood immediately so a priesthood of *rabbis* (literally, *great ones*) rose to the occasion, telling the people to tithe directly to them. This solved the need for funding, and it also solves the immediate need for spiritual leadership, but now there was a new problem, in that Yahweh's Torah does not recognize "rabbis." If the rabbis taught the people to obey Yahweh's Torah, then the people would reject the rabbis as impostors—and then they would go right back to assimilating into the Babylonian culture.

How could this dilemma be resolved? How could the rabbis teach the people to keep Torah, without being rejected as a result? The solution was that the rabbis had to redefine what the term *Torah* meant.

We understand that Yahweh gave His Torah to Moshe (Moses) at Mount Sinai. Since Yahweh's Torah is eternal, and unchanging, we obey it to the letter. However, the rabbis do not claim Yahweh's Torah is eternal. Rather, they claim Yahweh gave Moshe the authority to establish *Torah law* for his generation, and that this authority passes from generation to generation. According to this definition, *Torah law* can be whatever the great men (rabbis) in each generation say it should be. They also say that Moshe passed this authority on to Joshua, who passed it on to the judges, etc., until finally it came to rest on the rabbis. However, this is contrary to Yahweh's words.

> Devarim (Deuteronomy) 12:32
> 32 "Whatever I command you, be careful to observe it; you shall not add to it nor take away from it."

But if Yahweh says not to change His Torah, then why did the rabbis get the idea? Where did it come from? We can understand the rabbis much better if we realize that before the exile to Babylon, most of the rabbis were priests and Levites, and they were called on to make determinations in both legal and medical issues. For example, they had to determine the medical status of lepers.

Vayiqra (Leviticus) 13:9-14

9 "When the leprous sore is on a person, then he shall be brought to the priest.

10 And the priest shall examine him; and indeed if the swelling on the skin is white, and it has turned the hair white, and there is a spot of raw flesh in the swelling,

11 it is an old leprosy on the skin of his body. The priest shall pronounce him unclean, and shall not isolate him, for he is unclean.

12 "And if leprosy breaks out all over the skin, and the leprosy covers all the skin of the one who has the sore, from his head to his foot, wherever the priest looks,

13 then the priest shall consider; and indeed if the leprosy has covered all his body, he shall pronounce him clean who has the sore. It has all turned white. He is clean.

14 But when raw flesh appears on him, he shall be unclean."

The priests would approach this as a legal issue—and the fact that the priests had a legal orientation helps to explain why the rabbis see themselves as divinely inspired court justices. It also explains why they believe their opinions carry the weight of *Torah law*. The big problem is that they make the same mistake Havvah made. They have allowed the serpent to deceive them into believing that they are qualified to discern good and evil on their own (by their intellect), rather than hearing and obeying Yahweh's voice.

B'reisheet (Genesis) 3:4-5
4 Then the serpent said to the woman, "You will not surely die.
5 For Elohim knows that in the day you eat of it your eyes will be opened, and you will be like Elohim, knowing good and evil."

Like Havvah, the rabbis stopped listening to Yahweh's voice. They altered the definition of Torah from that of Yahweh's authority, to that of their own authority. The rabbis view the Torah as an important historical legal precedent that they can use to justify their own assumed authority. Perhaps that is why they don't want to go back to the Torah of Moshe—they would have to submit to Yahweh's Spirit (which is something that flesh does not like to do).

Instead of viewing Yahweh's Torah as a perfect marital covenant which is not to be altered, the rabbis teach that Jewish halachic law is an evolving field in which the more modern enactments of the scribes are far more important than the ancient rulings of Yahweh's Torah. In fact, they teach that while we can break the Torah (because there are "positive and negative precepts"), if we transgress the enactments of the scribes, we incur the penalty of death.

My son, be more careful in [the observance of] the words of the Scribes than in the words of the Torah, for in the laws of the Torah there are positive and negative precepts; but, as to the laws of the Scribes, whoever transgresses any of the enactments of the Scribes incurs the penalty of death.
[Babylonian Talmud, Tractate Eiruvin, 21b]

Because of their legal orientation, the rabbis assume that Eliyahu (Elijah) the prophet had a "court," and they say that even if Eliyahu (and his alleged court) were to disagree with their more recent majority rulings, no one should listen to him.

> A Court is unable to annul the decisions of another Court, unless it is superior to it in wisdom and numerical strength! Furthermore, Rabbah b. Bar Hanah has said in the name of R. Johanan: In all matters a Court can annul the decisions of another Court except the eighteen things [prohibited by the Schools of Hillel and Shammai], for even were Elijah and his Court to come [and declare them permitted] we must not listen to him! [Babylonian Talmud, Tractate Avodah Zarah 36a]

Prophets were always sent to get the people to turn back to Yahweh, keep His commandments, and obey His voice. The prophets heard Elohim's voice and spoke according to it. However, the rabbis tell the people, "Don't pay attention to the man who speaks according to Yahweh's voice. Pay attention to our voice instead."

The rabbis make up substitutes for everything Yahweh says to do. An everyday example of this is the rabbinic hand-washing ritual. In this rabbinic tradition, men must pour water over their hands before each meal, and say a ritual prayer. The rabbis likely adapted this from Exodus 30:17-21, which tells the priests to wash their hands and feet at the brazen laver as a statute forever in all of their generations.

Shemote (Exodus) 30:17-21
17 Then Yahweh spoke to Moshe, saying:

18 "You shall also make a laver of bronze, with its base also of bronze, for washing. You shall put it between the tabernacle of meeting and the altar. And you shall put water in it,
19 for Aharon and his sons shall wash their hands and their feet in water from it.
20 When they go into the tabernacle of meeting, or when they come near the altar to minister, to burn an offering made by fire to Yahweh, they shall wash with water, lest they die.
21 So they shall wash their hands and their feet, lest they die. And it shall be a statute forever to them — to him and his descendants throughout their generations."

We need to understand that obedience to the rabbinical commandments is referred to as obeying the "works of Torah." These are the same "works of Torah" the Apostle Shaul (Paul) refers to.

Galatim (Galatians) 2:15-16
15 We who are Jews by nature, and not sinners of the Gentiles,
16 knowing that a man is not justified by the works of the Torah but by faith in Yeshua Messiah, even we have believed in Messiah Yeshua, that we might be justified by faith in Messiah and not by the works of the Torah; for by the works of the Torah no flesh shall be justified.

What the rabbis are really suggesting is that the way to salvation is by submitting to their authority. This kind of authority is what Scripture refers to as a "yoke." Yeshua tells us to accept only His yoke, for His yoke is easy, and light.

Mattityahu (Matthew) 11:30

30 "For My yoke is easy and My burden is light."

The great struggle between Yeshua and the rabbis is the struggle of whose authority should be accepted. Time and again, the rabbis suggested that Yeshua should accept rabbinic authority—and time and again, Yeshua said that the main thing was not to obey the man-made teachings of the rabbis, but the commands that His Father gave.

Mattityahu (Matthew) 15:1-9
1 Then the scribes and Pharisees who were from Jerusalem came to Yeshua, saying,
2 "Why do Your disciples transgress the tradition of the elders? For they do not wash their hands when they eat bread."
3 He answered and said to them, "Why do you also transgress the commandment of Elohim because of your tradition?
4 For Elohim commanded, saying, 'Honor your father and your mother'; and, 'He who curses father or mother, let him be put to death.'
5 But you say, 'Whoever says to his father or mother, "Whatever profit you might have received from me is a gift to Elohim" —
6 then he need not honor his father or mother.' Thus you have made the commandment of Elohim of no effect by your tradition.
7 Hypocrites! Well did Isaiah prophesy about you, saying:
8 'These people draw near to Me with their mouth, And honor Me with their lips, But their heart is far from Me.
9 And in vain they worship Me, Teaching as doctrines the commandments of men.'"

Had the rabbis taught Yahweh's Torah (rather than man-made *Torah law*) Yeshua would probably have spoken in favor of them. However, because they taught a rabbinic replacement for Yahweh's Torah, Yeshua was not in favor.

But what did Yeshua mean when He said that the scribes and the Pharisees sit in Moshe's seat, and we should do what they say to do, even though we should not do according to their works?

Mattityahu (Matthew) 23:1-13
1 Then Yeshua spoke to the multitudes and to His disciples,
2 saying: "The scribes and the Pharisees sit in Moshe's seat.
3 Therefore whatever they tell you to observe, that observe and do, but do not do according to their works; for they say, and do not do.
4 For they bind heavy burdens, hard to bear, and lay them on men's shoulders; but they themselves will not move them with one of their fingers.
5 But all their works they do to be seen by men. They make their phylacteries broad and enlarge the borders of their garments.
6 They love the best places at feasts, the best seats in the synagogues,
7 greetings in the marketplaces, and to be called by men, 'Rabbi, Rabbi.'
8 But you, do not be called 'Rabbi'; for One is your Teacher, the Messiah, and you are all brethren.
9 Do not call anyone on earth your father; for One is your Father, He who is in heaven.
10 And do not be called teachers; for One is your Teacher, the Messiah.

11 But he who is greatest among you shall be your servant.

12 And whoever exalts himself will be humbled, and he who humbles himself will be exalted.

13 "But woe to you, scribes and Pharisees, hypocrites! For you shut up the kingdom of heaven against men; for you neither go in yourselves, nor do you allow those who are entering to go in."

In the first century, "Moshe's seat" was a literal physical chair where the scribes and the Pharisees sat and read the Torah scrolls aloud. It was like a modern-day pulpit. Yeshua said to do everything they said when they sat in Moshe's seat (and read the Torah aloud), because those words came from His Father. However, He also said not to do according to their *works*, because the "works of the Law" are nothing more than the majority opinions of the rabbis.

In verse 13, Yeshua said the scribes and the Pharisees shut up the kingdom of heaven against men. Not only did they refuse to go in, but they stopped others from entering in as well. That is, not only did they refuse to obey Yahweh's voice, they even taught others not to listen for Yahweh's voice (but instead they gave them the rabbinic "works of Torah" as a substitute for true obedience and sanctification).

Scripture is all about spirits, and the spirit on the rabbinic scribes and Pharisees gave Yahweh's people a substitute for hearing and obeying Yahweh's voice. Isn't that also what Satan did?

B'reisheet (Genesis) 3:4-5
4 Then the serpent said to the woman, "You will not surely die,

5 for Elohim knows that in the day you eat of it your eyes will be opened, and you will be like Elohim, knowing good and evil."

Earlier we saw how Jeremiah prophesied that Yahweh would bring the Jews back to the land after seventy years. However, after seventy years, 90 percent of the Jews did not want to go back home. Life was easier out in Babylon than it was in the land. The Jews had been given Babylonian citizenship, and many of them had taken Babylonian wives. If they stayed in Babylon, life would be easy—but if they went back home to the land, life would suddenly become very hard. Only those with a spirit to reject the Babylonian captivity and return to their inheritance in Israel would find this kind of a trade-off worthwhile.

In the days of Ezra and Nehemiah, 10 percent of the Jews decided to go back home to the land. The other 90 percent stayed out in the Babylonian captivity, and eventually became lost to history, being scattered into all the nations. From a physical standpoint both Jews and Ephraimites were now lost, but from a spiritual standpoint, they were both held captive by the enemy. It was as if Satan had taken their hearts captive by the pleasures of sin. This is why Yeshua said He came to proclaim liberty to the (spiritual) captives.

Luqa (Luke) 4:18
18 "The Spirit of Yahweh is upon Me, Because He has anointed Me to preach the Good News to the poor; He has sent Me to heal the brokenhearted, to proclaim liberty to the captives, and recovery of sight to the blind, To set at liberty those who are oppressed;"

Yet Yeshua did not come only for those who were lost out in the nations; He also came to set at liberty those who were spiritually oppressed by the rabbis. He came to set them at liberty from rabbinic custom. All of this is in keeping with Yeshua's role as the Messiah, whom Daniel said would come 7 weeks and 62 weeks (i.e., 69 weeks) after the command went forth for the Jews to restore and rebuild Jerusalem.

Daniel 9:25
25 "Know therefore and understand, that from the going forth of the command to restore and build Jerusalem until Messiah the Prince, there shall be seven weeks and sixty-two weeks. The street shall be built again, and the wall, even in troublesome times."

The Hebrew word for *weeks* is *shevua*, which means *seven*. If each *seven* represents seven earth years, then "Messiah the Prince" would come 483 years after the command went forth to restore and rebuild Jerusalem. History tells us that King Artaxerxes gave this command in 457 BCE. Four hundred and eighty three years after that brings us to 26 CE, which is the same year Yeshua began His ministry. This is just one proof of many that Yeshua is the prophesied "Messiah the Prince" of Daniel 9 (because no one else fits this historical description).

Strong's Hebrew Concordance tells us that the word *prince* in Daniel 9:25 is the Hebrew word *nagiyd* (נגיד), which refers to a commander who leads from the front. This word is of key importance in understanding who Yeshua is, and how we are to relate to Him.

OT:5057 nagiyd (naw-gheed'); or nagid (naw-gheed'); from OT:5046; a commander (as occupying the front), civil, military or religious; generally (abstractly, plural), honorable themes.

Many commentators have suggested that the reason the Pharisees rejected Yeshua is that He was not the military leader they had expected Messiah the Prince would be. Judea was under Roman control, and the Pharisees expected Messiah the Prince to unify the people, lead a military revolt, and throw the Romans out of the land. Instead, Yeshua launched a spiritual campaign which split the nation into two camps: the minority who had eyes to see (and ears to hear), and the majority that did not.

Mattityahu (Matthew) 10:34-39
34 "Do not think that I came to bring peace on earth. I did not come to bring peace but a sword.
35 For I have come to 'set a man against his father, a daughter against her mother, and a daughter-in-law against her mother-in-law';
36 and 'a man's enemies will be those of his own household.'
37 He who loves father or mother more than Me is not worthy of Me. And he who loves son or daughter more than Me is not worthy of Me.
38 And he who does not take his cross [stake] and follow after Me is not worthy of Me.
39 He who finds his life will lose it, and he who loses his life for My sake will find it."

As we saw in earlier chapters, the classic role of a messiah is that of someone who brings the lost and scattered of Israel back to the covenant, and leads them to victory over their enemies. However, it made no sense for Yeshua to throw the Romans out of the land, just so the anti-Torah rabbinical order could keep on misleading the people. Yeshua saw the rabbinical system to be as much of a threat to His people as the Roman army was (if not more so). At least the people could easily identify the Romans as an enemy, while they could not easily discern that the rabbis were propagating a deception. Perhaps that is why, rather than leading a military revolt against the Romans, Yeshua declared a spiritual war against the rabbis, to set Yahweh's people free from rabbinical oppression.

By the first century, the Levitical and priestly lineages had been lost, so they could not go back to the Levitical order. But if Yeshua was setting His people free from rabbinic oppression and deception, and it was not possible to go back to the old Levitical order, then how were the people to have the kind of spiritual leadership that it takes to have unity and cohesion as a nation? In the next chapter we will see how Yeshua established a new priesthood based on the order of Melchizedek, which was to take over from the rabbis, and further His kingdom worldwide.

The Renewed Melchizedekian Order

In the last chapter we saw how the Levitical order had no funding when the Jews went into Babylon—and therefore the Levitical order collapsed. Then we saw how the rabbinical order arose to take its place. This provided continuity of leadership, but it gave rise to a different problem in that the rabbis had to create a new substitute for the Torah in order to justify staying in power. Yet even though the rabbis created a substitute torah, Yahweh still gave them favor for a time, in order to fulfill His purposes. However, eventually Yahweh removed His favor from the rabbinical order, and He sent His son to raise up a renewed Melchizedekian order, to replace them.

There are several complexities and subtleties involved in the transposition of priesthoods that took place in the first century, so in order to understand what really took place (as well as what we are supposed to be doing today), let us take a brief overview of the history of Israel's priesthoods. This will lay the foundation for a much deeper, richer understanding in future chapters.

As we explain in *Torah Government*, there are three (or some say four) main roles (or offices) in Israel. These three (or four) main offices are:
1. The king (government)
2. The priest (spiritual government)
3. The prophet (Yahweh's spokesman)
4. The anointed judge (a combination of all three)

Some people believe we should restore the original ways of doing things, as they were done in the Garden of Eden. However, this is not what Scripture teaches.

Although the patriarchs originally filled all three or four offices, this cannot be the ultimate goal, because Israel is no longer just one nuclear family, but a nation of interdependent families. The need for organization and division of labor is increased, because there are many more people.

In Adam's time there was no division of labor. Adam's sons brought offerings to Yahweh by themselves. Hevel (Abel) brought Yahweh the first and finest of what Yahweh gave him, which pleased Yahweh. However, Qayin (Cain) just brought "an" offering (i.e., nothing special), and Yahweh was displeased.

> B'reisheet (Genesis) 4:3-5
> 3 And in the process of time it came to pass that Qayin brought an offering of the fruit of the ground to Yahweh.
> 4 Hevel also brought of the firstborn of his flock and of their finest. And Yahweh respected Hevel and his offering,
> 5 but He did not respect Qayin and his offering. And Qayin was very angry, and his countenance fell.

This passage is interpreted in different ways, but in verse 4, the word "finest" is the Hebrew word *chelev* (חלב). In context, this word refers to the richest or choicest part. This shows us that Yahweh likes it when we honor Him by giving the first and best parts back to Him (as Hevel did).

> OT:2459 cheleb (kheh'-leb); or cheleb (khay'-leb); from an unused root meaning to be fat; fat, whether literally or figuratively; hence, the richest or choice part:

There are many Hebrew word plays (puns) in Scripture. Hevel wanted to show Yahweh His love by giving Him the first and finest of what he had. This was a manifestation of Hevel's spirit. In Hebrew, the word for spirit is *ruach* (רוח). This is related to the Hebrew word for an aroma, which is *riach* (ריח). When we have a spirit (רוח) to serve Yahweh with our first and finest, it is a pleasing aroma (ריח) to Yahweh. This is the kind of spirit that pleases our Husband and King—and it was this same kind of spirit that Noach showed, which also pleased Yahweh.

> B'reisheet (Genesis) 8:21
> 21 And Yahweh smelled a soothing aroma (ריח). Then Yahweh said in His heart, "I will never again curse the ground for man's sake, although the imagination of man's heart is evil from his youth; nor will I again destroy every living thing as I have done."

Through Noach's time, the patriarchs were still offering to Yahweh by themselves. However, by Avram's day there was a separate priesthood. This was the start of the division of internal governance into three separate roles (king, priest, and prophet).

> B'reisheet (Genesis) 14:18-20
> 18 Then Melchizedek king of Shalem brought out bread and wine; he was the priest of Elohim Most High.
> 19 And he blessed him and said: "Blessed be Avram of Elohim Most High, Possessor of heaven and earth;
> 20 And blessed be Elohim Most High, Who has delivered your enemies into your hand." And he gave him a tithe of all.

It is sometimes said that division of labor is one of the principles upon which all advanced societies are built. Yahweh favors division of labor, because it leads to specialization—and with specialization, societies are more productive.

Yahweh favored Melchizedek and his priesthood, or Avram would not have given him a tithe. Avram's grandson Ya'akov (Jacob) also gave tithes, and probably tithed through the same Melchizedekian order as his grandfather had.

> B'reisheet (Genesis) 28:20-22
> 20 Then Ya'akov made a vow, saying, "If Elohim will be with me, and keep me in this way that I am going, and give me bread to eat and clothing to put on,
> 21 so that I come back to my father's house in peace, then Yahweh shall be my Elohim.
> 22 And this stone which I have set as a pillar shall be Elohim's house, and of all that You give me I will surely give a tenth to You."

Earlier we saw that while the patriarchs were alive, it was not necessary to develop separate government offices. However, as the patriarchs died and the tribes grew, they no longer had a single patriarch in common to unify them. This is the point at which it became necessary to develop separate offices, to keep the tribes from drifting apart. This is probably also why Yahweh sent the tribes into Egypt before Israel died. Pharaoh was a tyrant, but he was able to keep the tribes together under his strong central rule. Further, the time the tribes spent in bondage together under Pharaoh helped Israel develop a strong and enduring sense of identity as a people.

Because man's carnal nature is to rule (rather than to be ruled), men dislike submitting to anyone else (whether in government, or in priesthood). Men are always looking for ways to avoid submitting to their government, and to avoid supporting their priesthood. However, unless a nation has unified leadership and a centralized priesthood, the nation will fall, as Yeshua tells us that every kingdom (or nation) that is divided against itself cannot stand.

Mattityahu (Matthew) 12:25
25 But Yeshua knew their thoughts, and said to them: "Every kingdom divided against itself is brought to desolation, and every city or house divided against itself will not stand."

Before the tribes of Israel could come out from under Pharaoh's strong central *tyrant* leadership, first they needed to develop centralized *servant* leadership. For this reason, Yahweh sent Moshe (Moses), who would spend the rest of his life serving Yahweh and His people.

Now that Israel had its own government, Yahweh could give Israel its own priesthood. Because Yahweh had killed all the firstborn sons of Egypt, Yahweh claimed all of the firstborn of Israel for Himself.

Shemote (Exodus) 13:2
2 "Separate unto Me all the firstborn, whatever opens the womb among the children of Israel, both of man and beast; it is Mine."

The job of any priest is to uphold Yahweh's standards; and the order of the firstborn did not last long, as neither Aharon nor the firstborn restrained the people at the incident of the golden calf.

Shemote (Exodus) 32:25-26

25 Now when Moshe saw that the people were unrestrained (for Aharon had not restrained them, to their shame among their enemies),

26 then Moshe stood in the entrance of the camp, and said, "Whoever is on Yahweh's side — come to me!" And all the sons of Levi gathered themselves together to him.

The Levites showed themselves willing to oppose the people, and uphold Yahweh's standards. Thus, while the entire camp of Israel is set apart unto Yahweh, the Levitical priesthood is set apart a little more. Within that order, the priests are set apart even more. Next, the high priest is most set apart. Thus, while all Israel is set apart from the world, there still has to be an order within Israel, or nothing functions properly. However, Korah and the other men rose up against Yahweh's ordained order.

Bemidbar (Numbers) 16:1-3

1 Now Korah the son of Izhar, the son of Kohath, the son of Levi, with Dathan and Abiram the sons of Eliab, and On the son of Peleth, sons of Reuben, took men;

2 and they rose up before Moshe with some of the children of Israel, two hundred and fifty leaders of the congregation, representatives of the congregation, men of renown.

3 They gathered together against Moshe and Aharon, and said to them, "You take too much upon yourselves, for all the congregation is set apart, every one of them, and Yahweh is among them. Why then do you exalt yourselves above the assembly of Yahweh?"

Korah reasoned that the entire assembly was set apart, and that there should be no distinction between them. He sought to erase any distinction. Yahweh was very displeased, and Korah and his men paid for it with their lives (and the lives of their families).

Bemidbar (Numbers) 16:31-33
31 Now it came to pass, as he finished speaking all these words, that the ground split apart under them,
32 and the earth opened its mouth and swallowed them up, with their households and all the men with Korah, with all their goods.
33 So they and all those with them went down alive into the pit; the earth closed over them, and they perished from among the assembly.

Once Yahweh had established Moshe in the kingship, and the Levites in an internal priesthood, Yahweh began to refine and develop Israel's kingship. Moshe's father-in-law Yithro (Jethro) told Moshe that in addition to their division into twelve tribal armies, the people should be organized into subdivisions of tens, fifties, hundreds, and thousands. That is, in addition to gross divisions by tribes (analogous to what later became the Judeo-Christian nations), the people were also to be organized within their tribes (and later, their nations).

Shemote (Exodus) 18:21
21 "Moreover you shall select from all the people able men, such as fear Elohim, men of truth, hating covetousness; and place such over them to be rulers of thousands, rulers of hundreds, rulers of fifties, and rulers of tens."

As we mentioned earlier, the lost tribes later became the Christian kingships of Europe—and these Christian kingships had order and governance inside their own borders. They also established judicial functions within all of their gates, as Yahweh commands.

Devarim (Deuteronomy) 16:18
18 "You shall appoint judges and officers in all your gates, which Yahweh your Elohim gives you, according to your tribes, and they shall judge the people with just judgment."

Yahweh said Israel would one day have a king. The only caveat was that Yahweh said Israel should not choose a king *for themselves*, like all the other nations that were around them. Instead, they were to set over themselves the king (leader) of Yahweh's choosing.

Devarim (Deuteronomy) 17:14-15
14 "When you come to the land which Yahweh your Elohim is giving you, and possess it and dwell in it, and say, 'I will set a king over me like all the nations that are around me,'
15 you shall surely set a king over you whom YHWH your Elohim chooses; one from among your brethren you shall set as king over you; you may not set a foreigner over you, who is not your brother."

Israel could have asked for a set apart king, so they could be set apart; but they did exactly what Yahweh said not to do—they asked for a king so they could be like all the (other) nations. That is, they chose to be profane. This is a prophetic foreshadow of democracy, where the people choose their own leaders according to their own desires (rather than ask Yahweh to give them the leader He wants them to have). Notice how, in verse 5, Israel asks for a king so they can be like all the other nations.

172

Shemuel Aleph (1 Samuel) 8:4-5
4 Then all the elders of Israel gathered together and came to Samuel at Ramah,
5 and said to him, "Look, you are old, and your sons do not walk in your ways. Now make us a king to judge us like all the nations."

Verse 20 confirms that Israel's sin was not in seeking a set apart king (like David), but in seeking a non-set apart king, so they could be like all the other nations.

Shemuel Aleph (1 Samuel) 8:19-20
19 Nevertheless the people refused to obey the voice of Samuel; and they said, "No, but we will have a king over us,
20 that we also may be like all the nations, and that our king may judge us and go out before us and fight our battles."

Had the Israelites asked Shemuel (Samuel) for a set apart king, Yahweh would surely have been pleased.

Yahweh eventually gave Israel a righteous king, so that Yeshua could come from David's line. He was to become our High Priest in the heavens forever, according to the order of Melchizedek.

Ivrim (Hebrews) 6:19-20
19 This hope we have as an anchor of the soul, both sure and steadfast, and which enters the Presence behind the veil,
20 where the forerunner has entered for us, even Yeshua, having become High Priest forever according to the order of Melchizedek.

The term *Melchizedek* translates roughly as "King of Righteousness." This perfectly describes Yeshua, who fulfills not just the high priestly role, but also the role of the kingship (i.e., the commander of Yahweh's armies). This is a key core concept that we need to understand, if we are to realize who Yeshua is, and how He wants His bride to help Him during His absence.

In the last chapter we saw that Yeshua came to liberate those who were spiritually oppressed by the rabbis, as well as those who were in spiritual captivity in the nations (Ephraim, but in reality all twelve tribes—plus the lost and scattered seed of Avraham). What Yeshua came to begin was a generations-long spiritual campaign that would go through many phases—and because Yeshua would not be physically present to lead the spiritual war, He had to train up a priesthood to lead His army in His absence.

What so many people do not realize is that Yeshua did not want a ragtag, disorganized rabble, but a well-organized spiritual fighting force. His army would have to take the Good News to all four corners of the world, calling the lost and scattered children of Avraham and Israel back into the covenant through faith in Yeshua Messiah, uniting them as one cohesive nation, even though they would not have a country to call their own. This could only be done with some form of central organization and leadership. Just as in earlier times, centralized organization and leadership would be key to Israel's success. (Not coincidentally, this is why it is called the Melchizedekian order, and not the Melchizedekian disorder.)

Just as the Levites were ordered along military lines, the Melchizedekian priesthood would also need to be ordered along military lines. Yeshua would lead them, as their King and High Priest, through his priesthood—which is perhaps the reason He came to Yochanan HaMatbil (John the Baptist) to be immersed.

Mattityahu (Matthew) 3:13-17
13 Then Yeshua came from Galilee to Yochanan at the Jordan to be immersed by him.
14 And Yochanan tried to prevent Him, saying, "I need to be immersed by You, and are You coming to me?"
15 But Yeshua answered and said to him, "Permit it to be so now, for thus it is fitting for us to fulfill all righteousness." Then he allowed Him.
16 When He had been immersed, Yeshua came up immediately from the water; and behold, the heavens were opened to Him, and He saw the Spirit of Elohim descending like a dove and alighting upon Him.
17 And suddenly a voice came from heaven, saying, "This is My beloved Son, in whom I am well pleased."

Before a high priest is anointed, first he must be cleansed, just as Aharon and his sons had to be washed with water. This washing with water was basically the same idea as immersion (baptism).

Shemote (Exodus) 29:4
4 "And Aharon and his sons you shall bring to the door of the tabernacle of meeting, and you shall wash them with water."

Next came the anointing. With Aharon and his sons, the anointing was with blood and oil.

Shemote (Exodus) 29:21

21 "And you shall take some of the blood that is on the altar, and some of the anointing oil, and sprinkle it on Aharon and on his garments, on his sons and on the garments of his sons with him; and he and his garments shall be set apart, and his sons and his sons' garments with him."

Yeshua could not go to the rabbis to be anointed, because they did not truly follow Elohim (but their own authority). This is why He went to Yochanan HaMatbil to be anointed, as he was the son of Zechariah, a Levitical high priest.

Luqa (Luke) 1:13
13 But the messenger said to him, "Do not be afraid, Zechariah, for your prayer is heard; and your wife Elisheva will bear you a son, and you shall call his name Yochanan."

Once Yeshua had been immersed in water, then He was immersed by the Set apart Spirit (Matthew 3:16, above).

What so many people fail to grasp is that just as a king is the leader of a temporal (physical) army, the high priest is the leader of a spiritual army. These two are to work together to subdue the earth for Yahweh. In this light, let us look at the four main offices we listed at the start of this chapter, in military terms:

1. The king (leads the temporal army)
2. The priest (leads the spiritual army)
3. The prophet (communicates with Yahweh)
4. The anointed judge (a combination of all three)

As we will explain later, apostles are basically judges— except that while there is typically only one anointed

176

judge at a time, there can be any number of apostles. The only requirement is that they all work together as part of one cohesive spiritual army, after the order of Melchizedek. However, the thing so many people miss is that there has to be order between them. They have to submit one to another in the Spirit, and then together they must submit to Yahweh's word. If they do not submit both to Yahweh's Spirit and His word, then the result is chaos and confusion (which, as we will see later, is a decent operational definition of the Messianic Israel movement).

Once Yeshua had become anointed as the High Priest of the renewed Melchizedekian order, He immediately searched for twelve dedicated men who would eagerly lay down the rest of their lives for the privilege of joining His spiritual army, and organizing the people, so they could begin taking the spiritual battle to the enemy.

The Spectrum of Discipleship

As we will see, Yeshua established a high standard for His original twelve disciples—and yet there were other disciples in the first century who did not meet the same high standard Yeshua established. But how was that possible? To understand the answer to this question (and what it means for us today) let us look at what scholars call the law of first mention (or first use theory).

The law of first mention tells us that the first time a concept is introduced (or a commandment is given) in Scripture, it establishes a standard, or a precedent. All later variations will be judged by this standard. One obvious example of this is marriage. In Genesis 2, marriage was established as one man and one woman, married together for life (as one flesh).

> B'reisheet (Genesis) 2:23-24
> 23 And Adam said: "This is now bone of my bones And flesh of my flesh; She shall be called Woman, Because she was taken out of Man."
> 24 Therefore a man shall leave his father and mother and be joined to his wife, and they shall become one flesh.

While there are certain conditions where polygyny (plural wives) is lawful (and even commanded), it was not Yahweh's original intent. There is always a certain spiritual and physical cost associated with polygyny, because it deviates from the original standard of one wife for life. Even celibacy (which is in other ways an exalted ideal) carries certain costs, in that it is not good for human beings to be alone (because that deviates from Yahweh's original pattern).

Another example of the law of first mention is how, during the conquest of Canaan, Yahweh commanded that all spoils of war were to be utterly destroyed.

Devarim (Deuteronomy) 7:23-26
23 But Yahweh your Elohim will deliver them over to you, and will inflict defeat upon them until they are destroyed.
24 And He will deliver their kings into your hand, and you will destroy their name from under heaven; no one shall be able to stand against you until you have destroyed them.
25 You shall burn the carved images of their gods with fire; you shall not covet the silver or gold that is on them, nor take it for yourselves, lest you be snared by it; for it is an abomination to Yahweh your Elohim.
26 Nor shall you bring an abomination into your house, lest you be doomed to destruction like it. You shall utterly detest it and utterly abhor it, for it is an accursed thing.

However, during the conquest of Jericho, Achan the son of Carmi took forbidden spoils, and kept them for himself. This sin caused Israel to be defeated by the men of Ai. When this was discovered, Achan was put to death for disobeying Yahweh's command.

Yehoshua (Joshua) 7:18-26
18 Then he brought his household man by man, and Achan the son of Carmi, the son of Zabdi, the son of Zerah, of the tribe of Judah, was taken.
19 Now Joshua said to Achan, "My son, I beg you, give glory to Yahweh Elohim of Israel, and

make confession to Him, and tell me now what you have done; do not hide it from me."

20 And Achan answered Joshua and said, "Indeed I have sinned against Yahweh Elohim of Israel, and this is what I have done:

21 When I saw among the spoils a beautiful Babylonian garment, two hundred shekels of silver, and a wedge of gold weighing fifty shekels, I coveted them and took them. And there they are, hidden in the earth in the midst of my tent, with the silver under it."

22 So Joshua sent messengers, and they ran to the tent; and there it was, hidden in his tent, with the silver under it.

23 And they took them from the midst of the tent, brought them to Joshua and to all the children of Israel, and laid them out before Yahweh.

24 Then Joshua, and all Israel with him, took Achan the son of Zerah, the silver, the garment, the wedge of gold, his sons, his daughters, his oxen, his donkeys, his sheep, his tent, and all that he had, and they brought them to the Valley of Achor.

25 And Joshua said, "Why have you troubled us? Yahweh will trouble you this day." So all Israel stoned him with stones; and they burned them with fire after they had stoned them with stones.

26 Then they raised over him a great heap of stones, still there to this day. So Yahweh turned from the fierceness of His anger. Therefore the name of that place has been called the Valley of Achor to this day.

Achan's punishment for disobedience shows that the wages of sin is death. After Yahweh set this standard, He later allowed the children of Israel to keep the cattle and the spoils of war, so long as they destroyed the enemy king, and his city.

Yehoshua (Joshua) 8:1-2
1 Now Yahweh said to Joshua: "Do not be afraid, nor be dismayed; take all the people of war with you, and arise, go up to Ai. See, I have given into your hand the king of Ai, his people, his city, and his land.
2 And you shall do to Ai and its king as you did to Jericho and its king. Only its spoil and its cattle you shall take as booty for yourselves. Lay an ambush for the city behind it."

Modern militaries follow this same pattern when they set high standards for discipline during basic training. The standard of discipline can be relaxed once the recruits arrive at their unit, but if there are ever discipline problems, the standards can be reintroduced very quickly.

While most scholars realize the law of first mention plays out all through the Tanach (Old Testament), few realize that it also plays out in the Renewed Covenant (New Testament), with regard to disciples. In Luke 14:26-33, Yeshua tells us that in order to be His disciple we must hate our lives and our families, and bear our own burdens. We must also literally lay down our lives in this world, forsaking all that we have.

Luqa (Luke) 14:26-33
26 "If anyone comes to Me and does not hate his father and mother, wife and children, brothers and sisters, yes, and his own life also, he cannot be My disciple.
27 And whoever does not bear his cross [or stake] and come after Me cannot be My disciple.

28 For which of you, intending to build a tower, does not sit down first and count the cost, whether he has enough to finish it —
29 lest, after he has laid the foundation, and is not able to finish, all who see it begin to mock him,
30 saying, 'This man began to build and was not able to finish.'
31 Or what king, going to make war against another king, does not sit down first and consider whether he is able with ten thousand to meet him who comes against him with twenty thousand?
32 Or else, while the other is still a great way off, he sends a delegation and asks conditions of peace.
33 So likewise, whoever of you does not forsake all that he has cannot be My disciple."

When Yeshua invited the disciples to follow Him, they immediately dropped their nets (i.e., their lives in the world), and began seeking to help Him further His spiritual kingdom. This is a perfect expression of the law of first mention, in that it establishes a perfect high standard.

Mattityahu (Matthew) 4:18-22
18 And Yeshua, walking by the Sea of Galilee, saw two brothers, Shimon called Kepha, and Andrei his brother, casting a net into the sea; for they were fishermen.
19 Then He said to them, "Follow Me, and I will make you fishers of men."
20 They immediately left their nets and followed Him.
21 Going on from there, He saw two other brothers, James the son of Zebedee, and John his brother, in the boat with Zebedee their father, mending their nets. He called them,

22 and immediately they left the boat and their father, and followed Him.

Likewise, Yeshua told the rich young ruler that before he could enter the kingdom of Elohim, first he had to give up all of his physical possessions. He had to show that he valued the things of the Spirit more than he valued anything in the material world.

Mattityahu (Matthew) 19:16-30
16 Now behold, one came and said to Him, "Good Teacher, what good thing shall I do that I may have eternal life?"
17 So He said to him, "Why do you call Me good? No one is good but One, that is, Elohim. But if you want to enter into life, keep the commandments."
18 He said to Him, "Which ones?" Yeshua said, "'You shall not murder,' 'You shall not commit adultery,' 'You shall not steal,' 'You shall not bear false witness,'
19 'Honor your father and your mother,' and, 'You shall love your neighbor as yourself.'"
20 The young man said to Him, "All these things I have kept from my youth. What do I still lack?"
21 Yeshua said to him, "If you want to be perfect, go, sell what you have and give to the poor, and you will have treasure in heaven; and come, follow Me."
22 But when the young man heard that saying, he went away sorrowful, for he had great possessions.
23 Then Yeshua said to His disciples, "Assuredly, I say to you that it is hard for a rich man to enter the kingdom of heaven.
24 And again I say to you, it is easier for a camel to go through the eye of a needle than for a rich man to enter the kingdom of Elohim."

25 When His disciples heard it, they were greatly astonished, saying, "Who then can be saved?"
26 But Yeshua looked at them and said to them, "With men this is impossible, but with Elohim all things are possible."
27 Then Kepha answered and said to Him, "See, we have left all and followed You. Therefore what shall we have?"
28 So Yeshua said to them, "Assuredly I say to you, that in the regeneration, when the Son of Man sits on the throne of His glory, you who have followed Me will also sit on twelve thrones, judging the twelve tribes of Israel.
29 And everyone who has left houses or brothers or sisters or father or mother or wife or children or lands, for My name's sake, shall receive a hundredfold, and inherit eternal life.
30 But many who are first will be last, and the last first."

Other believers did something similar when they sold their excess lands and goods, and laid the funds at the apostles' feet, to be used for ministry.

Ma'asei (Acts) 4:34-35
34 Nor was there anyone among them who lacked; for all who were possessors of lands or houses sold them, and brought the proceeds of the things that were sold,
35 and laid them at the apostles' feet; and they distributed to each as anyone had need.

While some of the early disciples were required to sell all of their possessions, other disciples only had to sell *excess* houses and lands. This makes sense, in that most of the disciples were married, and they still needed a place to house their families (and guests).

Ma'asei (Acts) 21:16
16 Also some of the disciples from Caesarea
went with us and brought with them a certain
Mnason of Cyprus, an early disciple, with whom
we were to lodge.

In fact, at least one of Yeshua's disciples was rich, and
did not sell all of his things.

Mattityahu (Matthew) 27:57
57 Now when evening had come, there came a
rich man from Arimathea, named Joseph, who
himself had also become a disciple of Yeshua.

How can we understand these seeming contradictions?
According to the law of first mention, the original twelve
disciples met Yeshua's perfect standard. They literally
forsook all their physical possessions, and spent the
rest of their lives seeking to further His kingdom.
However, after this perfect standard was established, it
was then relaxed, so that those who were not called to
forsake all worldly possessions could still serve, to
whatever extent they felt led.

Christian scholarship commonly applies the following
four principles to discipleship:

1. Memorize Yeshua's words (learn)
2. Apply Yeshua's words to one's life (apply)
3. Imitate Yeshua (conform oneself to His words)
4. Make more disciples (replicate oneself)

To apply these principles 100 percent, we must lay
down all of our physical possessions, join the order of
Melchizedek, and spend the rest of our life actively
building Yeshua's kingdom. However, even if we do not

feel led to this extent, we can still apply these four principles to our lives. The reward is not as great, but this is how Joseph of Arimathea could still be a disciple without laying down all of his wealth. He simply applied these principles to the degree he felt led.

How can we know how much Elohim wants us to give to Him? The answer "simply give everything" is not necessarily correct. The correct answer is to pray, listen in the Spirit, and obey what we hear. If we do not abide in His Spirit (breath), then we are cut off from Him, and are of no use to Him. The key principle is to breathe, pray, and listen.

> Yochanan (John) 15:4-8
> 4 "Abide in Me, and I in you. As the branch cannot bear fruit of itself, unless it abides in the vine, neither can you, unless you abide in Me.
> 5 I am the vine, you are the branches. He who abides in Me, and I in him, bears much fruit; for without Me you can do nothing.
> 6 If anyone does not abide in Me, he is cast out as a branch and is withered; and they gather them and throw them into the fire, and they are burned.
> 7 If you abide in Me, and My words abide in you, you will ask what you desire, and it shall be done for you.
> 8 By this My Father is glorified, that you bear much fruit; so you will be My disciples."

If we pray and listen and obey what His Spirit (breath) tells us to do, then we are His disciples, to whatever extent (and in whatever capacity) He leads us. We are to do as we honestly feel led, knowing that we are answerable to Elohim alone.

Yeshua was a celibate Nazirite who laid down His time, His possessions, and His life to help bring back the lost and scattered children of Israel from their apostasy. He did not live His life for Himself, but for His brothers and sisters in Israel. He spent His life furthering His Father's kingdom here on earth. Because Yeshua's mission was to give all that He had, and because He followed through with His mission, His reward (and His love) is complete.

But what then shall we say about Avraham, or King David? Would they have received a better reward had they been celibate Nazirites? No, in truth they would have received less of a reward, because they would not be walking the path Yahweh chose for them. We should all be glad they did not try to be celibate, when Yahweh had called them to be fruitful and multiply, or else none of us would be here today.

What we see, then, are two legitimate paths for disciples. One is to join the priesthood full time, laying down all one's physical possessions, and going on the mission field (in whatever nation one is called). The other legitimate path is to raise up children in the way they should go, while supporting the priesthood financially, and also conducting local outreach. When the priesthood works internationally, and the rest of the disciples work locally, together we can bring more believers to Yeshua. We discuss this in more detail in *Fulfilling the Great Commission*.

What is Torah Really?

Yahweh is following a methodical plan to restore fallen mankind. The first step was to find a man who would obey His voice and save his family from a flood. The next step was to find a man who was willing to leave his home and his kin, and sojourn in a land that he had not known.

> B'reisheet (Genesis) 12:1-3
> 12 Now Yahweh had said to Avram: "Get out of your country, From your family And from your father's house, To a land that I will show you.
> 2 I will make you a great nation; I will bless you And make your name great; And you shall be a blessing.
> 3 I will bless those who bless you, And I will curse him who curses you; And in you all the families of the earth shall be blessed."

Avram's descendants went down into Egypt, where they were afflicted by Pharaoh; but this affliction served to unify them as a people. Then, after Israel's national identity was formed, Yahweh sent Moshe (Moses) to lead them out of Egypt, and give them a centralized government. Thus they were a nation under governance, even though they only had a promise of a land to call home.

In addition to a civil government, Yahweh gave Israel an organized priesthood to serve as their spiritual government. However, Israel did not realize that the goal was to hear and obey Yahweh's voice; so just like Adam and Havvah (Eve) who had disobeyed Yahweh's voice before them, the Israelites had to be sent out of Yahweh's land.

Ephraim went into spiritual captivity in Assyria, and Judah went into spiritual exile in Babylon; and although 10 percent of Judah came back to the land of Israel in the days of Ezra and Nehemiah, the rabbis kept them in spiritual oppression with their false version of Torah.

Messiah the Prince was sent to dispel this chaos. He declared spiritual war against the rabbis for misleading His people. Having received the anointing of the Spirit, He established a new priesthood based on the order of Melchizedek, so that His people would have clean leadership when they came to the truth.

Just as Avram had left his home and his father's house, Yeshua's priests would also leave their homes and their father's houses, and go into every nation on earth, to lands that Yahweh would show them by His Spirit. There they would make still more disciples to serve as a worldwide officer corps of His spiritual army, teaching them to do everything that Yeshua had told them.

Mattityahu (Matthew) 28:18-20
18 And Yeshua came and spoke to them, saying, "All authority has been given to Me in heaven and on earth.
19 Go therefore and make disciples of all the nations, immersing them in the name of the Father and of the Son and of the Set apart Spirit,
20 teaching them to observe all things that I have commanded you; and behold, I am with you always, even to the end of the age." Amein.

Some people believe the goal of our faith is simply to learn about Yeshua. This is a mistake. In fact, the goal of our faith is to become Yeshua's bride—and a bride is described as a helper. If we don't know that Yeshua was sent as a warrior Prince on a mission to raise a spiritual army and establish a literal kingdom here on earth (with the goal of subduing the earth), then we can never realize how to help Him, or please Him. All of our efforts will be in vain.

Yeshua was sent to take the spiritual war to the world, releasing the spiritual captives in every country. As it was in the days of Avraham, and as it was in the days of Moshe, the disciples would be a nation without a physical land to call home—and yet they still needed some form of unified spiritual government. Without such unified spiritual government, the movement would soon become leaderless and disoriented, which would make them easy prey for the enemy. This need to unify and operate as a single fighting force is why the spiritual temple is described as being built together on a single foundation of apostles and prophets (who serve as its leadership core).

> Ephesim (Ephesians) 2:19-22
> 19 Now, therefore, you are no longer strangers and foreigners, but fellow citizens with the saints and members of the household of Elohim,
> 20 having been built on the [single] foundation of the apostles and prophets, Yeshua Messiah Himself being the chief cornerstone,
> 21 in whom the whole building, being fitted together, grows into a [single] set apart temple in Yahweh,
> 22 in whom you also are being built together for a dwelling place of Elohim in the Spirit.

We already saw how Catholicism spread much faster outside the land of Israel than the Nazarene faith did, seeing as it promised eternal life without having to keep the Torah of Moshe. However, this issue of what it truly means to "keep Torah" is greatly misunderstood today. Since we cannot "keep" the Torah unless we understand what it means, let us spend some time exploring this topic in detail.

As we saw earlier, the term *torah* is often translated as *law*, because the instructions of our Creator carry the weight of law. However, this word translates directly as *instruction*. We also saw that there are three separate priesthoods mentioned in the Torah of Moshe (the first five books of Moses), and each of them has their own unique set of operating instructions (torah):

1. The Melchizedekian priesthood
2. The priesthood of the firstborn
3. The Levitical priesthood

Inside the Torah of Moshe are three separate operating torot (plural of torah). That is, when we are obeying the Torah of Moshe, we must be supporting either the Melchizedekian priesthood (which operates according to the Melchizedekian torah), the priesthood of the firstborn (which operates according to its torah), or the Levitical priesthood (which operates according to the Levitical torah). So long as we are supporting the active priesthood (which operates according to its own unique set of instructions), then we are obeying the Torah of Moshe.

We need to understand that the rules for operating inside of the land of Israel are very different from the rules for operating outside the land of Israel. Inside the land of Israel, the Levitical priesthood will likely be active, and the active torah will call us to bring animal sacrifices up to the temple three times a year. Outside the land of Israel, however, there is no such temple, and therefore no need to gather at it, since our primary mission is not to bring the family together for family reunions (i.e., festivals) three times a year. Our primary mission is to take the Good News to the lost and scattered children of Avraham and Israel, and bring them together as one in Yeshua Messiah.

In the last chapter we saw how Yeshua went to Yochanan HaMatbil (John the Immerser) in order to be ritually cleansed, so He could receive His anointing as the King and High Priest of the order of Melchizedek. At that time, the anointing passed from the rabbinical order to Yeshua's renewed order of Melchizedek. What we need to realize is that the instructions (torah) also changed at that time, because Yeshua's priesthood had a different mission than the Levitical order had. That is why Hebrews 7:12 tells us when the priesthood was changed, there was also (of necessity) a change in the active duty set of instructions (torah).

Ivrim (Hebrews) 7:12
12 For the priesthood being changed, of necessity there is also a change of the torah.

The rabbis have caused a lot of confusion by defining the Torah of Moshe as a checklist of 613 laws. This makes it sound like Yahweh gave Israel a checklist of 613 do's and don'ts, and as long as Israel did not violate any of those 613 laws, they would automatically be part of His bride. However, as we saw earlier, the rabbis gloss over the requirement to hear and obey Yahweh's still small spiritual voice (in favor of teaching the people to obey their majority opinion).

Contrary to what the rabbis teach, "keeping Torah" does not call for rigid obedience to a fixed checklist of laws. Rather, "keeping Torah" is a heart condition in which we eagerly seek to please our Husband by following His instructions. This may sound like a fine point of distinction, but it is critical that we understand it.

When a bride decides to come under her husband's covering, she makes a conscious decision to obey him. If her husband gives her one set of instructions today, and then he gives her a different set of instructions tomorrow (perhaps because the situation changes), she is not "keeping his instructions" if she insists on doing what he said to do yesterday. Rather, she only remains under her husband's covering if she accepts his new instructions (today).

When we submit to Yahweh, and accept His covering, this implies that we will obey His voice, both today and tomorrow (no matter where it leads, and no matter if our instructions change). If we insist on doing what He said to do in Egypt, but don't accept new direction in the Sinai, that is not keeping Torah.

Yahweh told the Israelites to dwell in the land He would give them. However, when Judah disobeyed Yahweh, Yahweh sent word through Jeremiah that they should go into Babylon, dwell there, and have children there.

Yirmeyahu (Jeremiah) 29:4-7
4 "Thus says Yahweh of hosts, the Elohim of Israel, to all who were carried away captive, whom I have caused to be carried away from Jerusalem to Babylon:
5 Build houses and dwell in them; plant gardens and eat their fruit.
6 Take wives and beget sons and daughters; and take wives for your sons and give your daughters

to husbands, so that they may bear sons and daughters — that you may be increased there, and not diminished.

7 And seek the peace of the city where I have caused you to be carried away captive, and pray to Yahweh for it; for in its peace you will have peace."

Yahweh never told Israel to seek the peace of Babylon in the first five books of Moshe—and yet this was His instruction (torah). Yet, some people are so dull, and so hard of hearing that they refuse to believe Yahweh said this, because it goes against what Yahweh said to do in the first five books of Moshe. They cannot seem to get beyond the concept that the first five books of Moshe are only a record of what Yahweh spoke unto Israel in the wilderness—and that what Yahweh really wants is for us to listen attentively to His voice at all times—for that is when we are truly under His instruction.

What gets confusing is that some of the instructions Yahweh gave at Mount Sinai were given as standing orders, and some were not. For example, when we live in the land, we are told to go up to Jerusalem three times a year. However, these standing orders do not apply when we live outside the land of Israel, or when we hear Yahweh's voice directing otherwise. The instructions can change, depending on the situation. To see what we mean by that, let us consider the example of traffic laws, and the traffic cop.

Today we have traffic laws—yet if a traffic cop directs us to go against the normal flow of traffic, we are still obeying the law, even if we are breaking the letter of it. This is a perfect analogy of how Yahweh's Spirit can order us to do something that is against the normal set of standing orders. For example, Yahweh commanded

Eliyahu (Elijah) to hide in the Wadi Qerith for a year. Even though the Wadi Qerith is inside the land of Israel, Eliyahu did not go up to Jerusalem for the feasts (because he was told to hide).

Melachim Aleph (1 Kings) 17:1-3
1 And Elijah the Tishbite, of the inhabitants of Gilead, said to Ahab, "As Yahweh Elohim of Israel lives, before whom I stand, there shall not be dew nor rain these years, except at my word."
2 Then the word of Yahweh came to him, saying,
3 "Get away from here and turn eastward, and hide by the Brook Qerith, which flows into the Jordan."

Any army has standing rules. For example, you may have a standing order to assemble at 06:00 hours; but if your commander says to do something else, you don't argue with him. Moreover, if your commander decides to give you a completely new and different set of standing orders because the war is moving into a new phase of operations, you don't argue—you just obey. This is what happened in the first century.

Among other reasons, Yahweh had commanded the people to come up to Jerusalem three times a year because He knew it would serve as a common experience that would unify the people. However, after Yeshua came, it was no longer time for the people to gather around a temple. Yeshua was not a Levite, and He had no authority over a renewed Levitical priesthood. Further, the Levitical lineages were lost, and Yeshua made no effort to re-establish them. Moreover, a Levitical priesthood needs a temple, and there would be no physical temple in the next phase of Yeshua's spiritual war campaign.

A physical temple helps to teach the people the need to obey the letter of Torah (and that the wages of sin is death). However, a physical temple can only serve a limited geographical area, and now it was time to go into all nations, making disciples in Yeshua's name, beginning to gather the lost and scattered children of Avraham and Israel out of the nations. This was a new and different phase of the spiritual war campaign, and it called for a new and different way of organizing. As difficult as it might be to understand, it called for a new and different set of operating instructions (a new torah).

Just as the Levitical priesthood had to be organized to operate as a single priesthood with peak efficiency, Yeshua's priests would have to be organized to operate efficiently. Thus, the same principles would govern the order of Melchizedek, as have operated all throughout Israel's history.

In the last chapter we saw that Elohim has carefully led Israel through a series of learning and growth steps. At just the right time He has given them separate offices for the king, the priest, and the prophet. There is also the office of the anointed judge, which is a special combination of all three.

1. The king (physical army)
2. The priest (spiritual army)
3. The prophet (communication with Yahweh)
4. The anointed judge (a combination of all three)

In *Fulfilling the Great Commission* we also explain that apostles are basically anointed judges for Renewed Covenant (New Testament) times. However, since there are numerous apostles, but they are all supposed to work together, there must be a means of providing order, so that there will be unity, and efficiency. This system of order is called the *fivefold ministry*, and it is a discipline which all fivefold ministers are required to obey.

In Ephesians 2:19-22 we are told that Yeshua's spiritual temple (i.e., His body) is to be built upon one foundation of apostles and prophets. This means they are all required to work together, as part of the same organization (and there is no option otherwise). To operate independently (as so many ministers do) is to break Scripture.

> Ephesim (Ephesians) 2:19-22
> 19 Now, therefore, you are no longer strangers and foreigners, but fellow citizens with the saints and members of the household of Elohim,
> 20 having been built on the [single] foundation of the apostles and prophets, Yeshua Messiah Himself being the chief cornerstone,
> 21 in whom the whole building, being fitted together, grows into a [one] set apart temple in Yahweh,
> 22 in whom you also are being built together for a dwelling place of Elohim in the Spirit.

To put it in simple terms, there is no such thing as a "Bible believing independent assembly," or a "Bible believing independent minister." Ephesians 2:19-22 requires all ministers to operate together on one single doctrinal foundation of apostles and prophets—and to do otherwise is to fly in the face of Ephesians 2:19-22.

These principles of organization and unified leadership are as essential today as they were in the day when Yahweh called Israel out of Egypt. It is by virtue of these immutable principles that Israel is able to operate as a unified fighting force. To break these principles is to break the glue that holds Elohim's army together, which is why it is so astounding that so many ministers (who say they work for Yahweh) are actually furthering Satan's agenda by operating independently, as rogues, rather than operating in unity.

In the next chapter we will see how the apostles also operated on this unified foundation when a question of doctrine arose in Acts 15.

Yeshua's United Bride

Earlier we saw how Yeshua gave His disciples a great commission to go into all nations, and raise up even more disciples. As we will see, these disciples were to serve as the officer corps of His unified spiritual army.

Mattityahu (Matthew) 28:18-20
18 And Yeshua came and spoke to them, saying, "All authority has been given to Me in heaven and on earth.
19 Go therefore and make disciples of all the nations, immersing them in the name of the Father and of the Son and of the Set apart Spirit,
20 teaching them to observe all things that I have commanded you; and lo, I am with you always, even to the end of the age." Amein.

Not only was Yeshua's army to preach the Good News to the spiritual captives of Judah and Ephraim in all nations, it was also to provide worldwide spiritual leadership among those who accepted Him.

But how were Yeshua's priests supposed to organize? In Ephesians 4, Shaul (Paul) tells us that Elohim Himself gave five different ministerial gifts, or callings: apostles, prophets, evangelists, pastors, and teachers. All of His ministers are to work together as one in what is called the fivefold ministry order.

Ephesim (Ephesians) 4:11-16
11 And He Himself gave some to be apostles, some prophets, some evangelists, and some pastors and teachers,

12 for the equipping of the set apart ones for the work of ministry, for the edifying of the body of Messiah,

13 till we all come to the unity of the faith and of the knowledge of the Son of Elohim, to a perfect man, to the measure of the stature of the fullness of Messiah;

14 that we should no longer be children, tossed to and fro and carried about with every wind of doctrine, by the trickery of men, in the cunning craftiness of deceitful plotting,

15 but, speaking the truth in love, may grow up in all things into Him who is the head — Messiah —

16 from whom the whole body, joined and knit together by what every joint supplies, according to the effective working by which every part does its share, causes growth of the body for the edifying of itself in love.

Yeshua's government is no different than our earthly governments—all different kinds of workers have to get the job done together.

If you are a great king, and you have 144,000 sheep, and you have twelve under-shepherds working for you, you want one of them to take the lead, and coordinate the actions of the other eleven. He can then assign those who are good with raising hay to make hay, assign those who are good with repairing barns and fixing fences to those tasks, and take those who are truly good with the sheep to tend the sheep from day to day. His overall concern is to look out for your best interests, but he does this by serving the needs of the rest of the under-shepherds, who in turn look out for the needs of the sheep. Organization plays a key role in making things happen at peak efficiency.

If there is no system for central organization, your under-shepherds will not be able to operate at peak efficiency. Instead they will end up bickering among themselves to see who gets control of what sheep. This does not lead to the shepherds caring for the sheep—it leads to an attitude of "every man for himself." This is the situation in the Protestant world today.

Everyone is better served when there is some form of central servant government. Not surprisingly, this is precisely what the fivefold ministry calls for. We are to organize by the fivefold until we all come to the unity of the faith (verse 13, above). This will not only create true unity within His body, but will also help us to grow and become more spiritually mature (i.e., more pleasing to Yeshua).

Satan hates the fivefold ministry precisely because it leads to more spiritually mature brides. Satan wants us to believe that all we need to do is sit and learn (and not do). If we want to please our Husband, and be taken in marriage, then the Great Commission and the fivefold ministry are not optional. If we do not perform the Great Commission by way of the fivefold ministry, then we are not obeying our Husband (and hence, we cannot expect to be taken in marriage).

Yeshua told His followers that if they merely heard what Yeshua said to do, but did not do it, they would be like a man who built his house on the sand—and great would be the fall of his house.

Luqa (Luke) 6:46-49
46 "But why do you call Me 'Adon, Adon,' but not do the things which I say?

203

47 Whoever comes to Me, and hears My sayings and does them, I will show you whom he is like:

48 He is like a man building a house, who dug deep and laid the foundation on the rock. And when the flood arose, the stream beat vehemently against that house, and could not shake it, for it was founded on the rock.

49 But he who heard and did nothing is like a man who built a house on the earth without a foundation, against which the stream beat vehemently; and immediately it fell. And the ruin of that house was great."

If we want to be taken in marriage, we have to uphold our part of the marital covenant. That is, we not only have to learn what our Husband wants us to do—we also have to do it, and eagerly, so when Yeshua returns, He is pleased.

Yeshua wants us to work together, as a whole. This is not easy, but unity in the body is not optional. Shaul likens Yeshua's body to a human body, and no human body can survive if its parts are not in contact with each other (to the point where there is an exchange of bodily fluids). Schisms in the body do not please Yeshua.

Qorintim Aleph (1 Corinthians) 12:13-26

13 For by one Spirit we were all immersed into one body — whether Jews or Greeks, whether slaves or free — and have all been made to drink into one Spirit.

14 For in fact the body is not one member but many.

15 If the foot should say, "Because I am not a hand, I am not of the body," is it therefore not of the body?

16 And if the ear should say, "Because I am not an eye, I am not of the body," is it therefore not of the body?

17 If the whole body were an eye, where would be the hearing? If the whole were hearing, where would be the smelling?

18 But now Elohim has set the members, each one of them, in the body just as He pleased.

19 And if they were all one member, where would the body be?

20 But now indeed there are many members, yet one body.

21 And the eye cannot say to the hand, "I have no need of you"; nor again the head to the feet, "I have no need of you."

22 No, much rather, those members of the body which seem to be weaker are necessary.

23 And those members of the body which we think to be less honorable, on these we bestow greater honor; and our unpresentable parts have greater modesty,

24 but our presentable parts have no need. But Elohim composed the body, having given greater honor to that part which lacks it,

25 that there should be no schism in the body, but that the members should have the same care for one another.

26 And if one member suffers, all the members suffer with it; or if one member is honored, all the members rejoice with it.

In past centuries, the papacy held immense power over the Christian nations. If the pope excommunicated a Christian king for misbehavior, that king could lose his kingdom. Even though the papacy abused this power, this is the kind of authority that Scripture calls for.

Some are afraid of unity because of past abuses. They claim that we should not be organized or unified because the church is organized and unified. To support their argument, they often cite Revelation 18:4, which tells us to come out of the church, lest we share in her sins and receive of her plagues.

Hitgalut (Revelation) 18:4
4 And I heard another voice from heaven saying, "Come out of her, my people, lest you share in her sins, and lest you receive of her plagues."

The problem with this argument is that organization and unity are not what makes a church. In fact, there are many churches which have no leadership or organization. Rather, what defines a church is false doctrine (replacement theology). Further, we should not avoid organization, because Scripture commands that we organize. Ephesians 2:20 tells us Yeshua's temple is supposed to be built on one foundation of apostles and prophets.

Ephesim (Ephesians) 2:19-22
19 Now, therefore, you are no longer strangers and foreigners, but fellow citizens with the saints and members of the household of Elohim,
20 having been built on the [single] foundation of the apostles and prophets, Yeshua Messiah Himself being the chief cornerstone,
21 in whom the whole building, being fitted together, grows into a [singular] set apart temple in Yahweh,
22 in whom you also are being built together for a dwelling place of Elohim in the Spirit.

In *Fulfilling the Great Commission* we explain that the reason the apostolic foundation is supposed to be made up of apostles and prophets is precisely because these are the two classes of ministers who are able to hear Yahweh's voice. This is the key to everything. If we diligently heed the voice of Yahweh, then we know how to obey Yeshua's Melchizedekian torah; and if we do not heed His voice (but are led by our own intellect), then we are simply making another legalistic religion of man. Relying on the human mind did not work for the Pharisees, and it won't work for us either.

Kepha (Peter) tells us that Yeshua's house of worship is to be built of living stones, which hear and obey His voice.

> Kepha Aleph (1 Peter) 2:4-6
> 4 Coming to Him as to a living stone, rejected indeed by men, but chosen by Elohim and precious,
> 5 you also, as living stones, are being built up a spiritual house, a set apart priesthood, to offer up spiritual sacrifices acceptable to Elohim through Yeshua Messiah.
> 6 Therefore it is also contained in the Scripture, "Behold, I lay in Zion A chief cornerstone, elect, precious, And he who believes on Him will by no means be put to shame."

To build a stone temple, first one lays the foundation, and then one puts up walls. Once the roof is on, there is a space inside where people can come and worship. This analogy describes how Yeshua's fivefold ministers are to work together. Once the apostles and prophets have come together to form the apostolic foundation, the evangelists, pastors, and teachers must join with the apostles and prophets, and take their places on that apostolic foundation. Only when they all come together in order is a living temple built, where people can come and worship.

It is not okay for Yeshua's ministers to establish *independent* ministries any more than it would have been okay for Levitical priests to set up independent (and competing) temples in Jerusalem. The only way Yahweh would be pleased is if all of the priests and Levites operated together, under the direction of the earthly high priest. Anything other than that would not have been effective, or efficient—and it would not have led to unity within the nation.

As long as we are in the dispersion, there will certainly be more than one place to worship, but the leadership needs to work together. That is the only way we can remain one body, one nation, one people, and therefore, one unified fighting force.

In the next chapters we will see how the apostles all pulled together to keep the people united under one doctrine, even though they were in many different nations of the world.

Acts 15 and Rabbinic Authority

In earlier chapters we saw how Israel had a centralized government and an organized Levitical priesthood while it was still in the wilderness. This shows we can have an organized priesthood when we are outside of the land. Let us bear this in mind.

We also saw how Messiah the Prince came to take the spiritual campaign to restore fallen Adam into a new phase. The focus would no longer be on offering animal sacrifices in a temple, but on sending disciples into all nations to establish a global Melchizedekian priesthood. This worldwide Melchizedekian priesthood would call the lost and scattered children of Avraham and Israel out of every family and every clan. Then, generations later, a remnant of them would begin a slow return to their inheritance in Israel.

Further, we learned that the Levitical priesthood had no inheritance in the land. Likewise, Yeshua said that in order to be His disciple (i.e., a Melchizedekian priest), a man had to forsake all that he had. This was the price of serving Him and His people.

> Luqa (Luke) 14:33
> 33 "So likewise, whoever of you does not forsake all that he has cannot be My disciple."

Although the priests were not to have any possessions, the ministry would still need funding in order to carry out the Great Commission, so the people sold their possessions (Acts 2 and 4), and gave the proceeds to the apostles.

Ma'asei (Acts) 4:32-35

32 Now the multitude of those who believed were of one heart and one soul; neither did anyone say that any of the things he possessed was his own, but they had all things in common.

33 And with great power the apostles gave witness to the resurrection of the Adon Yeshua. And great favor was upon them all.

34 Nor was there anyone among them who lacked; for all who were possessors of lands or houses sold them, and brought the proceeds of the things that were sold,

35 and laid them at the apostles' feet; and they distributed to each as anyone had need.

If the apostles were not to have any inheritance, then why were the funds laid at the apostles' feet? For any organization to be effective, its leadership must be able to direct how the funds are spent. This is true whether we are talking about government, a business, a Melchizedekian priesthood, or whatever.

For the Levitical priesthood to work, the high priest had to have control of the funds. If the people simply gave their tithes, gifts, and offerings to the first priest they met (or to the priest that helped them offer their sacrifices), the temple service would quickly break down. It would be similar to paying a waiter at the restaurant, and allowing him to take all the money home. The manager would have no funds to pay the cooks and the dishwashers, or pay the grocery bill. The restaurant would soon be forced to close.

Unless the people all gave their tithes to the high priest (or his designee), the high priest would have no funds to distribute to those who chopped wood, or baked the showbread. Everyone with supporting jobs would have to abandon their posts, and work as altar priests. They would have to be there to meet the pilgrims as they came up to Jerusalem. But if everyone was a priest, and no one drew water, chopped wood, or baked showbread, the temple service would come to a halt. This is roughly analogous to the situation in Messianic Israel today. There is no separated priesthood, no real accountability, and no order.

In Acts 6 we see both organization and order. In those days, a complaint arose against the Hebrews by the Hellenists because the Hellenic widows had not been well taken care of. The apostles' response was to assign seven additional men to look after the widows. This was possible because the apostolic foundation had the power to direct how the funds were spent.

Ma'asei (Acts) 6:1-4
1 Now in those days, when the number of the disciples was multiplying, there arose a complaint against the Hebrews by the Hellenists, because their widows were neglected in the daily distribution.
2 Then the twelve summoned the multitude of the disciples and said, "It is not desirable that we should leave the word of Elohim and serve tables.
3 Therefore, brethren, seek out from among you seven men of good reputation, full of the Set apart Spirit and wisdom, whom we may appoint over this business;
4 but we will give ourselves continually to prayer and to the ministry of the word."

The reason Yahweh wants the apostolic foundation to have control of the funds is that, by definition, apostles and prophets hear Yahweh's voice. It is only by hearing and obeying Yahweh's voice, moment by moment, that they can know how Yahweh wants His funds spent.

The idea is that the evangelists, pastors, and teachers are supposed to realize that the apostles and prophets are hearing and obeying Yahweh's voice. They are to seek them for direction and counsel. However, when the evangelists, pastors, and teachers don't know what it is to hear Yahweh's voice, they do not feel a need to seek out the apostles and prophets, or operate on the apostolic foundation. This causes instant disunity, as in the Messianic world today.

Some believers distrust the very idea of an apostolic foundation. This is perhaps attributable to the fact that there has been so much abuse of power by the church. They are perhaps like wives who have been through a bad marriage, and who now distrust marriage. However, just because one makes a wrong choice of spouse, does that make the institution of marriage bad? Or does it mean they just made a poor choice of mate?

While the Catholic Church has a foundation of apostles and prophets, it is not a foundation of true apostles and true prophets. Like the rabbis, the Catholic leadership does not follow Yahweh's voice, but their own thoughts. This makes them blind guides, for as we saw earlier with Havvah (Eve) in the Garden of Eden, Satan's primary tactic is to get us to follow our own thoughts, rather than listen for Yahweh's voice. This is why we are told to take every thought into captivity to the obedience of the Messiah (and His Spirit).

Qorintim Bet (2 Corinthians) 10:3-6
3 For though we walk in the flesh, we do not war according to the flesh.

4 For the weapons of our warfare are not carnal but mighty in Elohim for pulling down strongholds,
5 casting down arguments and every high thing that exalts itself against the knowledge of Elohim, bringing every thought into captivity to the obedience of Messiah,
6 and being ready to punish all disobedience when your obedience is fulfilled.

Yahweh gave us brains, and He wants us to use them. However, we are first to abide in Yeshua, and then to think—and not the other way around. If at any time we forget to abide in Yeshua, then we will end up chasing after our own thoughts (and hence, we become Satan's spiritual captives).

Hearing and obeying Yahweh's voice is foundational to our faith. Those with the apostolic and prophetic gifts must listen continually for Yahweh's voice. In fact, this is why they are entrusted with leadership. If listening to Yahweh's words is not their top priority, then they are not living up to their office (and this is where both the rabbis and the church go wrong).

We know the offices of apostles and prophets are still for today, because Ephesians 4:13 tells us to organize according to the fivefold giftings until we all come to the unity of the faith.

Ephesim (Ephesians) 4:13
13 till we all come to the unity of the faith and of the knowledge of the Son of Elohim, to a perfect man, to the measure of the stature of the fullness of Messiah;

Further, Revelation 18:20 tells the apostles and prophets to rejoice over Babylon at her fall.

Hitgalut (Revelation) 18:20
20 "Rejoice over her, O heaven, and you set apart apostles and prophets, for Elohim has avenged you on her!"

Since the fall of Babylon is still a future event, we know that there will be apostles and prophets in the future—so we know that the offices of apostles and prophets are still for today.

Since apostles and prophets are those who listen for Yahweh's voice at all times, and since these offices are still for today, then those who are called to these offices must practice hearing and obeying His voice at all times. That is part of their job.

But what does all of this have to do with Acts 15?

Up through Acts 9, the Good News was being revealed to Jews only. However, in Acts 10, Yahweh showed Kepha (Peter) a vision of a great sheet descending from heaven, which was filled with unclean animals (which are symbolic of the gentiles).

Ma'asei (Acts) 10:9-16
9 The next day, as they went on their journey and drew near the city, Kepha went up on the housetop to pray, about the sixth hour.
10 Then he became very hungry and wanted to eat; but while they made ready, he fell into a trance
11 and saw heaven opened and an object like a great sheet bound at the four corners, descending to him and let down to the earth.

12 In it were all kinds of four-footed animals of the earth, wild beasts, creeping things, and birds of the air.

13 And a voice came to him, "Rise, Kepha; kill and eat."

14 But Kepha said, "Not so, Adon! For I have never eaten anything common or unclean."

15 And a voice spoke to him again the second time, "What Elohim has cleansed you must not call common."

16 This was done three times. And the object was taken up into heaven again.

The church teaches us that this vision means the clean food laws of Leviticus 11 no longer apply (and that we can now eat anything). However, Kepha tells us that it meant we should not call any man common or unclean. After Yeshua's sacrifice, the Great Commission was to be shared with every family and every clan in all nations—so we were not to avoid witnessing to others.

Ma'asei (Acts) 10:28

28 Then he said to them, "You know how unlawful it is for a Jewish man to keep company with or go to one of another nation. But Elohim has shown me that I should not call any man common or unclean."

Kepha said it is "unlawful" for a Jewish man to keep company with, or go to, one of another nation. This is not found in the Torah of Moshe, but is instead a rabbinical ruling. That Kepha would repeat a rabbinical ruling says something about him. If we couple this with the fact that Shaul's (Paul's) ministry was to the gentiles, while Kepha's ministry (up to this point) was to the *circumcised* (i.e., rabbinical Pharisees), it gives us an interesting picture of who Kepha truly was.

Kepha obeyed the Spirit's command to go to Cornelius' house, and six men of "the circumcision" (believing Pharisees) went with him. Kepha, then, was "hanging with the believing Pharisees." Yet while he preached, the Spirit fell on everyone who heard—and "those of the circumcision who believed were astonished."

> Ma'asei (Acts) 10:44-45
> 44 While Kepha was still speaking these words, the Set-apart Spirit fell upon all those who heard the word.
> 45 And those of the circumcision who believed were astonished, as many as came with Kepha, because the gift of the Set-apart Spirit had been poured out on the Gentiles also.

Rabbinical Pharisees believe gentiles can only convert to Judaism by following a specific legal process. In the first century this was called the *custom* of Moshe (as opposed to the Torah of Moshe). Today this is called the *Giur* (gee-yure) process. In the Giur process, new converts must first take classes to learn the rabbinic interpretation of Torah law. Then, after they have been indoctrinated into the rabbinic teachings, they are allowed to become physically circumcised. In the rabbinic mind, if they have obeyed the rabbinic procedure, they are submitted to rabbinic authority, and they are therefore now in Yahweh's favor (i.e., they are saved). This is why the circumcision was astonished when Yahweh poured out His Spirit on uncircumcised gentiles (like Cornelius and his house), who were not following the rabbinic traditions at all.

Men are very protective of their power and position, so when Kepha came back to Judea, the rabbinical circumcision contended with him there.

Ma'asei (Acts) 11:1-3

1 Now the apostles and brethren who were in Judea heard that the Gentiles had also received the word of Elohim.

2 And when Kepha came up to Jerusalem, those of the circumcision contended with him,

3 saying, "You went in to uncircumcised men and ate with them!"

Kepha explained the whole thing from the beginning, about how Elohim had shown him that he was not to call any man common or unclean, and how Yahweh had poured out the Spirit on Cornelius and his house. Then he asked them if they wanted him to try to stand up against what Elohim was doing.

Ma'asei (Acts) 11:15-18

15 "And as I began to speak, the Set-apart Spirit fell upon them, as upon us at the beginning.

16 Then I remembered the word of the Master, how He said, 'Yochanan indeed immersed with water, but you shall be immersed with the Set-apart Spirit.'

17 If therefore Elohim gave them the same gift as He gave us when we believed on the Adon Yeshua Messiah, who was I, that I could withstand Elohim?"

18 When they heard these things they became silent; and they glorified Elohim, saying, "Then Elohim has also granted to the Gentiles repentance to life!"

After these things, Yahweh poured out His Spirit on a great many Hellenized (Reform) believers in Antioch (who also were not obeying the rabbinic customs)—so the apostles sent Bar Naba (Barnabas) there.

Ma'asei (Acts) 11:19-25

19 Now those who were scattered after the persecution that arose over Stephen traveled as far as Phoenicia, Cyprus, and Antioch, preaching the word to no one but the Jews only.

20 But some of them were men from Cyprus and Cyrene, who, when they had come to Antioch, spoke to the Hellenists, preaching the Master Yeshua.

21 And the hand of Yahweh was with them, and a great number believed and turned to the Master.

22 Then news of these things came to the ears of the ecclesia in Jerusalem, and they sent out Bar Naba to go as far as Antioch.

23 When he came and had seen the grace of Elohim, he was glad, and encouraged them all that with purpose of heart they should continue with Yahweh.

24 For he was a good man, full of the Set-apart Spirit and of faith. And a great many people were added to the Master.

25 Then Bar Naba departed for Tarsus to seek Shaul.

It is amazing how stubborn and stiff necked men can be when their power and position is at stake. Even though Yahweh had clearly shown that He did not respect rabbinic authority in the case of Cornelius, the believing Pharisees still came to Antioch and told the Hellenized believers there that unless they followed the rabbinic Giur process, they could not be saved. In this passage the Giur process is called the custom of Moshe (as opposed to the Torah of Moshe). In verse 5 these rabbinic believers are called the "sect of the Pharisees who believed." This is the same spiritual group as the rabbinical "circumcision who believed."

Ma'asei (Acts) 15:1-2

1 And certain men came down from Judea and taught the brethren, "Unless you are circumcised according to the [rabbinic] custom of Moshe [i.e., Giur process], you cannot be saved."

2 Therefore, when Shaul and Bar Naba had no small dissension and dispute with them, they determined that Shaul and Bar Naba and certain others of them should go up to Jerusalem, to the apostles and elders, about this question.

It was a two or three week walk to go up from Antioch to Jerusalem, and we have to remember that in ancient times, road travel could be dangerous. There were often bandits and thieves—yet Shaul and Bar Naba seem to have felt that the prospect of doctrinal unity was worth the trip. It seems to have been important to them that all of the shepherds lead their sheep the right way. This may be because sheep follow their under-shepherds—and unless all of the under-shepherds lead the sheep in the same direction, the flock will soon be divided. (That is to say, Messiah's body will be split.)

Ma'asei (Acts) 15:4-5

4 And when they had come to Jerusalem, they were received by the ecclesia and the apostles and the elders; and they reported all things that Elohim had done with them.

5 But some of the sect of the Pharisees who believed rose up, saying, "It is necessary to circumcise them, and to command them to keep the Torah of Moshe."

The order suggested by the rabbinical believers is the same as the order of the rabbinic Giur Process:

1. Teach them the rabbinic interpretation of Torah
2. Circumcise them according to rabbinic ritual
3. Keep the rabbinic torah law

Earlier we saw that the rabbinical order arose from the Levitical order, whereas Yeshua's priesthood was to be based on the Melchizedekian order. That being the case, it would not work to allow the rabbis to assert rabbinic (i.e., Levitical) authority inside the order of Melchizedek; yet the rabbis were tenacious, and would not give up their presumed authority easily. We should note here that these rabbinical Pharisees who believed are analogous to the rabbinic Messianic Jews of today. These are Jews who have accepted Yeshua as the Messiah, still believe in rabbinic authority, and believe the Talmud is authoritative. This is ironic, since Yeshua never had anything good to say either about the rabbinical order, or about their man-made traditions and teachings (Talmud).

After there had been "much dispute," Kepha rose up to say that Yahweh had chosen him to deliver the Good News to the gentiles, and that he had not imposed rabbinic authority; therefore, why did the rabbis seek to put a rabbinic yoke on the necks of the new believers, when Yeshua had called them all out from under rabbinical authority? After all, they hoped to be saved by favor (grace) through faith themselves.

Ma'asei (Acts) 15:6-11
6 Now the apostles and elders came together to consider this matter.
7 And when there had been much dispute, Kepha rose up and said to them: "Men and brethren, you know that a good while ago Elohim chose among us, that by my mouth the Gentiles should hear the word of the Good News and believe.

8 So Elohim, who knows the heart, acknowledged them by giving them the Set apart Spirit, just as He did to us,

9 and made no distinction between us and them, purifying their hearts by faith.

10 Now therefore, why do you test Elohim by putting a yoke [rabbinic tradition] on the neck of the disciples which neither our fathers nor we were able to bear?

11 But we believe that through the favor of the Adon Yeshua Messiah we shall be saved in the same manner as they."

Then Shaul and Bar Naba related all of the miracles and wonders Elohim was doing among the gentiles (who were not submitted to rabbinic authority).

Ma'asei (Acts) 15:12
12 Then all the multitude kept silent and listened to Bar Naba and Shaul declaring how many miracles and wonders Elohim had worked through them among the Gentiles.

Ya'akov (James) then said that he judged they should not "trouble" the returning gentiles by placing a yoke of rabbinic authority on them, but that they could enter the assemblies simply by abstaining from four things Yahweh says will get one "cut off" from the nation (idolatry, sexual immorality, strangled [or unclean] meats, and blood). Ya'akov judged that if the gentiles would simply abstain from these four things, then they could enter the assemblies, where they could hear the Torah of Moshe being read aloud. In that way, the returning Jews and Ephraimites would come into compliance with Yahweh's word (as opposed to being indoctrinated in the rabbis' legal traditions).

Ma'asei (Acts) 15:13-21

13 And after they had become silent, Ya'akov answered, saying, "Men and brethren, listen to me:

14 Shimon has declared how Elohim at the first visited the Gentiles to take out of them a people for His name.

15 And with this the words of the prophets agree, just as it is written:

16 'After this I will return and will rebuild the tabernacle of David, which has fallen down; I will rebuild its ruins, and I will set it up;

17 So that the rest of mankind may seek Yahweh, even all the Gentiles who are called by My name, says Yahweh who does all these things.'

18 "Known to Elohim from eternity are all His works.

19 Therefore I judge that we should not trouble those from among the Gentiles who are [re]turning to Elohim,

20 but that we write to them to abstain from things polluted by idols, from sexual immorality, from things strangled, and from blood.

21 For Moshe has had throughout many generations those who preach him in every city, being read in the synagogues every Sabbath."

Notice Ya'akov's use of the word *judge* in verse 19. In Hebrew this word refers to something that apostles and prophets normally do.

As we explain in *Torah Government*, a *prophet* is someone who hears Yahweh's voice, and speaks what he hears Yahweh saying. This is also how the anointed judges of the Tanach (Old Testament) would render their judgments. They would hear the case, and then they would listen for Yahweh's voice, so they could know what the judgment was. That way, the judgment was not their own private interpretation, but it was the word that Yahweh had spoken. Not surprisingly, this is also how Yeshua says He judged (by speaking what He heard from above, rather than speaking according to His own will).

Yochanan (John) 5:30
30 "I can of Myself do nothing. As I hear, I judge; and My judgment is righteous, because I do not seek My own will but the will of the Father who sent Me."

There are three main offices in Israel: the king (the army), the priest (the spiritual army), and the prophet (communication with Yahweh). Anointed judges had to be a combination of all three because they led the nation in times when there was no king. Apostles are basically Renewed Covenant (New Testament) judges because they also fulfill all three roles.

One difference between anointed judges and apostles is that while there was only one anointed judge at a time when Israel was inside the land, there had to be more than one apostle at any given time because the Melchizedekian order had to go into every nation on earth. Because it was to be a unified priesthood, there had to be order between the apostles. This order was established by submitting first to Yahweh's Spirit, and then submitting one to another, and letting Yahweh's Spirit decide who is to take what position. However, as a practical matter, someone had to take the lead position, and in those days it was Ya'akov.

Some scholars believe Ya'akov was chosen to lead the assembly because he was Yeshua's half-brother. The only problem with this is that Yeshua had other half-brothers. Rather, what seems to make more sense is that Ya'akov was chosen to lead because he listened to the voice of the Spirit, and hence he showed wisdom. However, the key thing to notice here is that he said he *judged*, which in Hebrew means he believed he was speaking according to Yahweh's voice.

Not only had Yeshua condemned rabbinic authority, but the apostolic foundation also overturned the rabbis' assertions in Acts 15. The rabbis are an extension of the old Levitical order, and the Levitical order has no authority in the order of Melchizedek.

Different groups explain Acts 15 different ways, so let us be clear: Acts 15 determined that before the lost Jews and Ephraimites could join themselves to Yeshua's body, and join the nation, they must first abstain from idolatry, sexual immorality, strangled (or unclean) meats, and blood. If they did not abstain from these things, they could not enter the assemblies, because it would be defiling the camp. (Note that leadership could still meet with them on the outside.)

It appears that the apostles were attempting to identify the proper means of allowing the lost and scattered tribesmen to come back to the nation, without defiling the assembly. However, since it was the Catholic Church that ultimately went on to establish the Melchizedekian order worldwide, let us turn now, and look at the overall trends shaping the Catholic Church, and her Protestant daughters. Along the way we will see some surprising things, including a number of ways Satan hopes to trip us all up, and steal our crowns.

Keep Seeking Yeshua's Face

Revelation 12:13-17 says that when the dragon (Satan) saw that he had been cast to earth, he persecuted the woman (true Israel) who gave birth to the male child (Yeshua). The woman was given two wings of a great eagle, so that she might fly into the wilderness to her place. There she is nourished for a time and times and half a time, from the presence of the serpent. In *Revelation and the End Times*, we show how this symbolizes true Israel's flight from the false doctrines of the Catholic Church, which attempted to "wash away" the true believers with a flood of false doctrines.

Hitgalut (Revelation) 12:13-17
13 Now when the dragon saw that he had been cast to the earth, he persecuted the woman who gave birth to the male Child.
14 But the woman was given two wings of a great eagle, that she might fly into the wilderness to her place, where she is nourished for a time and times and half a time, from the presence of the serpent.
15 So the serpent spewed water [unclean doctrines] out of his mouth like a flood after the woman, that he might cause her to be carried away by the flood.
16 But the earth helped the woman, and the earth opened its mouth and swallowed up the flood which the dragon had spewed out of his mouth.
17 And the dragon was enraged with the woman, and he went to make war with the rest of her offspring, who keep the commandments of Elohim and have the testimony of Yeshua Messiah.

The woman survived, but now she wants to get back to the original apostolic faith. It is the same story as the prodigal son who wants to return home to his Father's house, just in a different parable.

> Luqa (Luke) 15:17-19
> 17 "But when he came to himself, he said, 'How many of my father's hired servants have bread enough and to spare, and I perish with hunger!
> 18 I will arise and go to my father, and will say to him, "Father, I have sinned against heaven and before you,
> 19 and I am no longer worthy to be called your son. Make me like one of your hired servants."'

As we saw earlier, Ephraim got tired of feeding the pigs (symbolic of idols in the Catholic Church). Coming to himself, he decided to humble himself and return home to his Father's house, no matter what the cost. However, it does no good for Ephraim to come part of the way home. If he stops before he returns to the original faith, and rests in the false doctrines (waters) of replacement theology, it is as if he has been swept away by Satan's flood.

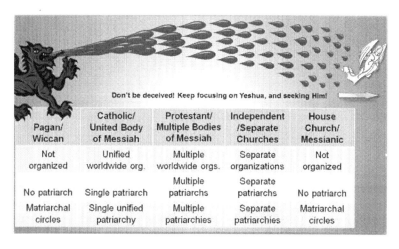

Don't be deceived! Keep focusing on Yeshua, and seeking Him!

Pagan/ Wiccan	Catholic/ United Body of Messiah	Protestant/ Multiple Bodies of Messiah	Independent /Separate Churches	House Church/ Messianic
Not organized	Unified worldwide org.	Multiple worldwide orgs.	Separate organizations	Not organized
No patriarch	Single patriarch	Multiple patriarchs	Separate patriarchs	No patriarch
Matriarchal circles	Single unified patriarchy	Multiple patriarchies	Separate patriarchies	Matriarchal circles

In visions, water represents the Spirit and doctrine. However, the dragon's water represents false spirits and tainted doctrines. Satan hopes the woman will be satisfied by false spirits and tainted doctrines, so that she will stop struggling to get back to the original faith.

Yehudah (Jude) 3
3 Beloved, while I was very diligent to write to you concerning our common salvation, I found it necessary to write to you, exhorting you to contend [struggle] earnestly for the faith which was once for all delivered to the saints.

The English word *contend* is the Greek *epagonizomai*, which means *to struggle for*.

NT:1864 epagonizomai (ep-ag-o-nid'-zom-ahee); from NT:1909 and NT:75; to struggle for: KJV - earnestly contend foreign

In the Aramaic Peshitta, the word *contend* is *d'agunah* (דאגונא), and it also means *to struggle*, but in a military sense. Therefore, we are to do more than just believe on Him. We, as His spiritual army, are to struggle to advance His faith around the globe. While anyone can say they love Yeshua, only those who truly love Him will be willing to struggle and make personal sacrifices to re-establish the original faith, and advance it around the globe, as the Melchizedekian order was always called to do. This is the narrow and afflicted path we are all called to walk.

Mattityahu (Matthew) 7:13-14
13 "Enter by the narrow gate; for wide is the gate and broad is the way that leads to destruction, and there are many who go in by it.

14 Because narrow is the gate and difficult is the way which leads to life, and there are few who find it."

Historically, the bride (who is called out of paganism) began traveling the narrow and afflicted path back to her Jewish Husband. However, most pilgrims stopped traveling at Catholicism. Catholicism formed a rest stop along the trail, where too many pilgrims became comfortable, so to speak. From there a minority of the pilgrims moved on, but most of those stopped within Protestantism. A minority of the pilgrims then moved on to independent Christianity, and now some are moving on to the house church and Messianic movements.

Those in the house church movement tell us that we do not need a separated priesthood, because we can all read Scripture for ourselves. This is like the argument that Korah and his men made when they told Moshe that because the entire assembly was set apart, there was no need for leadership.

Bemidbar (Numbers) 16:1-3
1 Now Korah the son of Izhar, the son of Kohath, the son of Levi, with Dathan and Abiram the sons of Eliab, and On the son of Peleth, sons of Reuben, took men;
2 and they rose up before Moshe with some of the children of Israel, two hundred and fifty leaders of the congregation, representatives of the congregation, men of renown.
3 They gathered together against Moshe and Aharon, and said to them, "You take too much upon yourselves, for all the congregation is set apart, every one of them, and Yahweh is among them. Why then do you exalt yourselves above the assembly of Yahweh?"

The house church argument is kind of like saying that because we can all read, our army does not need any leadership. This argument is illogical, and makes no sense. Nonetheless, house churches are the fastest growing part of the Christian church today.

The Sabbath version of the house church movement is called *Messianic Israel*, and it has the same flaws as the house church movement. In fact, as we compare and contrast the groups in the chart of the bride's flight, we will see some interesting patterns. (We have reprinted the same chart below.)

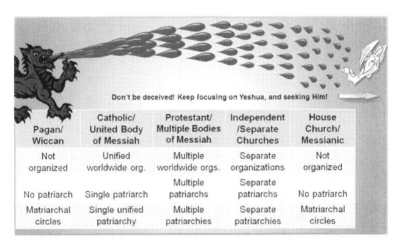

Don't be deceived! Keep focusing on Yeshua, and seeking Him!

Pagan/ Wiccan	Catholic/ United Body of Messiah	Protestant/ Multiple Bodies of Messiah	Independent /Separate Churches	House Church/ Messianic
Not organized	Unified worldwide org.	Multiple worldwide orgs.	Separate organizations	Not organized
No patriarch	Single patriarch	Multiple patriarchs	Separate patriarchs	No patriarch
Matriarchal circles	Single unified patriarchy	Multiple patriarchies	Separate patriarchies	Matriarchal circles

There are many differences among Catholics, Protestants, independent Christians, and those in the house church movement. However, they are all united in that they all practice a substitute for the original Nazarene faith. And as we look a little closer, we will see some fascinating trends.

The Catholics practice a kind of fivefold organization, but are told not to study Scripture for themselves. They are not told what it means to have an abiding personal relationship with Yeshua, nor are they taught to hear and obey His voice. However, while their level of knowledge is low and their relationship with the Spirit is often stunted, the level of obedience to the Great Commission and fivefold order in the Catholic Church is very high.

On the opposite end of the spectrum, those in the house churches study Scripture, and many of them have a personal relationship with the Messiah; but they typically reject fivefold order, and ignore the Great Commission. To them, *worship* is all about learning and fellowship. Most of them have no idea that we are called to form a unified spiritual army, and expand our Husband's kingdom. Unlike Catholicism, the level of knowledge in the house churches is high, but their level of obedience to the fivefold ministry and the Great Commission is almost nonexistent.

The Sabbath version of the house church movement is called Messianic Israel. Messianics are often mistaken for Nazarenes, but Messianic and Nazarene Israel are two distinct belief sets (and two distinct spirits).

Like the house church movement, the Messianics say that we do not need leadership, because we can read Scripture for ourselves. There is typically no real commitment to fulfilling the Great Commission (as the Messiah commanded). Instead it is all about reading, resting, and fellowshipping.

The Messianics know that our High Priest belongs to the order of Melchizedek, but they focus on learning the Levitical torah. In fact, many of them reject the Great Commission, based on the fact that it is not commanded explicitly in the Torah of Moshe.

Ironically, while the Messianics claim to "keep Torah," in practice what this means is that they rest on the Sabbath and festivals. They typically reject all forms of organization, leadership, accountability, and mission. While they think of themselves as Israelites, they hardly resemble Israel in the wilderness, or the first century Nazarenes.

Wilderness	Nazarenes	Messianic Israel
Levitical	Melchizedekian	Merchant vendors
Organized	Organized	Disorganized
Patriarchal	Patriarchal	Matriarchal circles
Leadership	Leadership	"Whatever"
Accountability	Accountability	Anarchy
United nation	United nation	No nation
Shepherd led	Shepherd led	Sheep led
Mission focus	Mission focus	Fellowship focus

From a standpoint of knowledge, Messianism is better than Catholicism. Messianism teaches an Israelite identity, and the correct calendar. It also avoids pope worship. However, in terms of obedience, Messianism is inferior to both Catholicism and Protestantism in that the Messianics well know that the Torah of Moshe commands order, discipline, and accountability—and yet they refuse to do that. They also refuse to obey the Great Commission, as Yeshua asks—and yet they expect to be taken as His bride.

Are the Messianics better than the Christians in knowing that both the Torah and Yeshua call for organization and leadership, and yet they refuse to do that? Is that not rather a sin?

Ya'akov (James) 4:17
17 Therefore, to him who knows to do good and does not do it, to him it is sin.

If the Catholics are perhaps like unto an ignorant bride, at least she is hard working, and faithful to what she does know. In contrast, if the Messianics are a well-educated bride, she is lazy, and slothful. She only wants to read about her Husband, but she does not want to help Him. She only wants to rest on His festival days, eat His spiritual food, and talk. Helping Him with the Great Commission is the farthest thing from her mind.

We might further subdivide the Messianic movement into *spiritualist* Messianics, *legalistic* Messianics, and *listening* Messianics. The last of these classes is best.

Unreached (unborn)	Christians (all kinds)	Messianic Judaism/Messianic Israel		
		Spiritualist, focus on spirits	Legalist, focus on points of law	Listen for Yahweh's voice
Not born again	Spiritual babies	Spiritually young	Spiritually young	Spiritually maturing
Need Messiah	Accept lawless Greek "Jesus"	Accept mixed Jesus-Yeshua	Rigid version of Hebrew Yeshua	Abide in Yeshua 24/7
No Torah	Lawless, false Torah	Mixed names, mixed dates, mixed Torah	Condemn those who have less knowledge	Humbly love and encourage others in Torah
Open to demonic spirits	Accept lawless Xtian spirit	Accept mixed spirits/spiritism (profane fire)	Harsh spirit, condemnation, legalistic spirit	Humbly seek to love and encourage all
Demonic rites and rituals	Modified order of Melchizedek	Modified order of Levi (wrong)	Modified order of Levi (wrong)	Assist order of Melchizedek

Spiritualist Messianics might be described as having one foot still in the church. They may keep Sabbath and festivals, but they are not very devout. They might mix the Hebrew and Hellenic names, calling Yeshua "Jesus," and equating Yahweh with "the Lord" (Ba'al), etc. They might also halfheartedly follow the food laws. From a certain standpoint we might look at them as "new recruits" to Yeshua's spiritual army, who need continuing training and encouragement (and we should take care not to discourage them in any way).

There are also (non-rabbinical) *legalistic* Messianics. These might be thought of as having *both* feet in Israel (which is good). The only problem is that they have harsh, judgmental attitudes (i.e., spirits). (*Attitude* is an English word that means close to the same thing as the Hebraic conception of a *spirit*, except that a spirit is a living thing.) Legalistic Messianics intellectually know that love is the heart of the Torah, but their attitude (spirit) does not reflect that. Even if they have no rabbinical leanings whatsoever, they are very much like the Pharisee in the parable of the tax collector.

> Luqa (Luke) 18:10-14
> 10 "Two men went up to the temple to pray, one a Pharisee and the other a tax collector.
> 11 The Pharisee stood and prayed thus with himself, 'Elohim, I thank You that I am not like other men — extortioners, unjust, adulterers, or even as this tax collector.
> 12 I fast twice a week; I give tithes of all that I possess.'
> 13 And the tax collector, standing afar off, would not so much as raise his eyes to heaven, but beat his breast, saying, 'Elohim, be merciful to me a sinner!'
> 14 I tell you, this man went down to his house justified rather than the other; for everyone who exalts himself will be humbled, and he who humbles himself will be exalted."

The final group is the most hopeful. A *listening* (or *broken*) Messianic realizes we have no righteousness to speak of. They realize that we are called to empty ourselves in total humility and brokenness, handing over control of our lives to His Spirit, and allowing Him to move us 24/7. Whether such listening Messianics understand Scripture perfectly or not, the fact that they listen to His Spirit is a very good sign. These are the most likely to convert to Nazarene Israel (although converts come from all over).

Over the course of centuries, Yeshua's Spirit has continued to call His bride out of the nations—yet the prospective brides respond in varying degrees. Many of those responding to His call came into Catholicism, while fewer came into Protestantism. Fewer still came into the house church movement, as they sought more knowledge and intimacy with their Husband. Then a minority of the house church has come into Messianic Israel, as they realized the importance of the Sabbath, the festivals, the set apart names, and their Israelite identities. Now some of the Messianics are beginning to realize that they also need to find the next level, because in order to do the Great Commission (as our Husband asks), we must act upon what we know.

Satan's job is to stop us from getting back to the original faith (and to our Husband) by washing us away with a flood of lies. If we accept any of his lies, or fail to act upon what we know, then we will never return back to the original faith, and our Husband will not delight in us.

Ishmael in the End Times

Adam and Havvah (Eve) fell from Yahweh's favor for failing to obey His voice. After this, Yahweh set in motion a multi-step plan of redemption involving all of Avraham's descendants.

As we saw earlier, Yahweh made a special covenant with Avraham because he obeyed Yahweh's voice.

> B'reisheet (Genesis) 22:15-18
> 15 Then the messenger of Yahweh called to Avraham a second time out of heaven,
> 16 and said: "By Myself I have sworn, says Yahweh, because you have done this thing, and have not withheld your son, your only son —
> 17 blessing I will bless you, and multiplying I will multiply your descendants as the stars of the heaven and as the sand which is on the seashore; and your descendants shall possess the gate of their enemies.
> 18 In your seed all the nations of the earth shall be blessed, because you have obeyed My voice."

While the covenant would come down through Israel (whose descendants included Ephraim and Judah), there was also a blessing given to Avraham's other son, Ishmael.

> B'reisheet (Genesis) 17:19-20
> 19 Then Elohim said: "No, Sarah your wife shall bear you a son, and you shall call his name Yitzhak; I will establish My covenant with him for an everlasting covenant, and with his descendants after him.

20 And as for Ishmael, I have heard you. Behold, I have blessed him, and will make him fruitful, and will multiply him exceedingly. He shall beget twelve princes, and I will make him a great nation [religious group]."

As we saw earlier, in Scripture, one's nationality is one's religion—so when Yahweh said He would make Ishmael a great "nation," He meant He would give him a great religion (Islam). While Islam is not "great" in terms of Scriptural accuracy, Islam is great in terms of sheer numbers—and in its end time role.

Yahweh does not care about our flesh, and so ethnicity means nothing to Him. However, Yahweh historically uses certain groups of people to accomplish certain tasks for Him. While Yahweh used Judah to bring forth Messiah, He used Ephraim to spread the worship of a Jewish Messiah around the globe. He is also using Ishmael to maintain the Semitic ideals of theocracy and corporate discipline (which are nearly lost in Ephraimite and Jewish culture).

But what is the relationship between Ishmael and his brother Yitzhak's (Isaac's) other son Esau? If Ishmael represents Muslims of all races, Esau (Edom) represents the ethnic Arabs (many of whom are also Islamic). These ethnic Arabs descend from Esau, who despised his birthright.

Genesis 25:29-34
29 Now Ya'akov cooked a stew; and Esau came in from the field, and he was weary.
30 And Esau said to Ya'akov, "Please feed me with that same red stew, for I am weary." Therefore his name was called Edom.

31 But Ya'akov said, "Sell me your birthright as of this day."
32 And Esau said, "Look, I am about to die; so what is this birthright to me?"
33 Then Ya'akov said, "Swear to me as of this day." So he swore to him, and sold his birthright to Ya'akov.
34 And Ya'akov gave Esau bread and stew of lentils; then he ate and drank, arose, and went his way. Thus Esau despised his birthright.

While today there are Muslims in all ethnic groups, Islam first arose among the Arabs (who descend from Esau). This may be because Genesis 28:8-9 tells us Esau married Ishmael's daughter Mahalath.

B'reisheet (Genesis) 28:8-9
8 Also Esau saw that the daughters of Canaan did not please his father Yitzhak.
9 So Esau went to Ishmael and took Mahalath the daughter of Ishmael, Avraham's son, the sister of Nebajoth, to be his wife in addition to the wives he had.

Genesis 36:3 tells us that Esau also married Ishmael's daughter Basemath.

B'reisheet (Genesis) 36:1-3
1 Now this is the genealogy of Esau, who is Edom.
2 Esau took his wives from the daughters of Canaan: Adah the daughter of Elon the Hittite; Aholibamah the daughter of Anah, the daughter of Zibeon the Hivite;
3 and Basemath, Ishmael's daughter, sister of Nebajoth.

After a few generations, Ishmael's and Esau's genetics became so intermixed that some people wrongly consider *Arab* and *Muslim* to be synonyms.

In Genesis 27:39 we are told that Esau would receive a blessing of the *shemen* (שמן) of the earth. This term is often translated as *fatness*, but it also translates as *oil*. This blessing explains why the (Islamic) Arab nations have abundant petroleum resources.

Genesis 27:39-40	
39 Then Yitzhak his father answered and said to him [Esau]: "Behold, your dwelling shall be of the fatness [oil] of the earth, And of the dew of heaven from above. 40 By your sword you shall live, And you shall serve your brother; And it shall come to pass, when you become restless, That you shall break his yoke from your neck."	(39) וַיַּעַן יִצְחָק אָבִיו וַיֹּאמֶר אֵלָיו ׀ הִנֵּה מִשְׁמַנֵּי הָאָרֶץ יִהְיֶה מוֹשָׁבֶךָ וּמִטַּל הַשָּׁמַיִם מֵעָל: (40) וְעַל חַרְבְּךָ תִחְיֶה וְאֶת אָחִיךָ תַּעֲבֹד ׀ וְהָיָה כַּאֲשֶׁר תָּרִיד וּפָרַקְתָּ עֻלּוֹ מֵעַל צַוָּארֶךָ

Verse 40 explains the many historical examples of how both Ephraimites and Jews have dominated Esau, and how Esau has risen up, and broken the Ephraimite and Jewish yoke from their neck. Some see the success of the spread of Islam, and also the 2012 Arab Spring, as an example of this prophecy.

While there are two houses in Israel, Yeshua tells us the kingdom of heaven is like leaven, which a woman took and hid in three measures of meal until it all was leavened.

Mattityahu (Matthew) 13:33
33 Another parable He spoke to them: "The kingdom of heaven is like leaven, which a woman took and hid in three measures of meal till it was all leavened."

If meal is ground seed, then these three measures of meal are the three main groups of Avraham's seed: Judah, Ephraim, and Ishmael. In Matthew 16:5-12, Yeshua tells us that leaven symbolizes false doctrine, and all three groups (Judah, Ephraim, and Ishmael) are now leavened with false doctrine.

Mattityahu (Matthew) 16:5-12
5 Now when His disciples had come to the other side, they had forgotten to take bread.
6 Then Yeshua said to them, "Take heed and beware of the leaven of the Pharisees and the Sadducees."
7 And they reasoned among themselves, saying, "It is because we have taken no bread."
8 But Yeshua, being aware of it, said to them, "O you of little faith, why do you reason among yourselves because you have brought no bread?
9 Do you not yet understand, or remember the five loaves of the five thousand and how many baskets you took up?
10 Nor the seven loaves of the four thousand and how many large baskets you took up?
11 How is it you do not understand that I did not speak to you concerning bread? — but to beware of the leaven of the Pharisees and Sadducees."

12 Then they understood that He did not tell them to beware of the leaven of bread, but of the doctrine of the Pharisees and Sadducees.

The false doctrines of Judaism, Christianity, and Islam will eventually be burned out by the fire of the great tribulation, but let us be careful to see that although each of these faiths gets some things wrong, they also get some things right. That is, the reason that Yeshua likens the kingdom of heaven to three measures of meal is that each measure of meal embodies an essential aspect of the kingdom—and it is therefore these three measures of Avrahamic meal that Yahweh is using to leaven the whole lump called earth.

If we were to depict the three Avrahamic faiths on an archer's target, they would cluster around the center of the target.

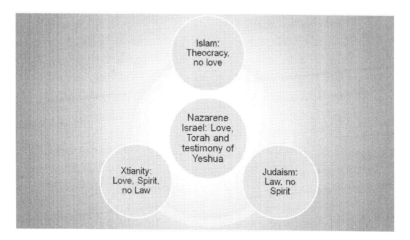

The word *torah* (תורה) is based on the root word *yarah* (ירה), which means *to point out* (as if to instruct). However, it also means *to shoot*, as if shooting at a archer's target (or a goal).

OT:3384 yarah (yaw-raw'); or (2 Chronicles 26:15) yara' (yaw-raw'); a primitive root; properly, to flow as water (i.e. to rain); transitively, to lay or throw (especially an arrow, i.e. to shoot); figuratively, to point out (as if by aiming the finger), to teach:
KJV - (+) archer, cast, direct, inform, instruct, lay, shew, shoot, teach (-ering), through.

The idea of flowing is that of letting the Spirit flow through us without obstruction. That is, our actions should flow from a pure, unquenched spirit, without taking anything in the material world (family, money, status, etc.) into account. When we are so in tune with Yahweh that His Spirit flows freely through us, and we obey His voice instinctively, then we are hitting the target (i.e., keeping the Torah). If we do anything other than that, then we are missing the target.

The Hebrew word for missing the target is *chata* (חטא), and this is the word for "sin" (i.e., missing the target). We miss the target when we take our focus off Yeshua, quench His Spirit, and fail to obey Elohim's voice (for whatever reason).

OT:2398 chata' (khaw-taw'); a primitive root; properly, to miss; hence (figuratively and generally) to sin; by inference, to forfeit, lack, expiate, repent, (causatively) lead astray, condemn.

Judaism, Islam, and Christianity all miss the mark in that they all have the wrong idea of who Elohim is, and what He wants. They also have the wrong idea of what it means to obey Yahweh's voice. Our goal, then, is to realize who Elohim truly is, and what He truly wants— and to obey His voice in all things. This is how we can

241

become more pleasing to Him (and not surprisingly, this is also the best way to survive the tribulation).

Some people counsel fighting against the New World Order. This is not wise. Yahweh is completely in charge, and if we resist what Yahweh is doing to leaven the whole lump of earth, then we will be found fighting against Elohim.

Ma'asei (Acts) 5:34-39
34 Then one in the council stood up, a Pharisee named Gamaliel, a teacher of the Torah held in respect by all the people, and commanded them to put the apostles outside for a little while.
35 And he said to them: "Men of Israel, take heed to yourselves what you intend to do regarding these men.
36 For some time ago Theudas rose up, claiming to be somebody. A number of men, about four hundred, joined him. He was slain, and all who obeyed him were scattered and came to nothing.
37 After this man, Judas of Galilee rose up in the days of the census, and drew away many people after him. He also perished, and all who obeyed him were dispersed.
38 And now I say to you, keep away from these men and let them alone; for if this plan or this work is of men, it will come to nothing;
39 but if it is of Elohim, you cannot overthrow it — lest you even be found to fight against Elohim."

Yahweh is perfectly in charge, and Yahweh knows what He is doing. At some point there will be a great war in the Middle East. After this war, our Ishmaelite cousins will convert to the worship of Elohim.

Yeshayahu (Isaiah 19:21-25

242

21 Then Yahweh will be known to Egypt, and the Egyptians will know Yahweh in that day, and will make sacrifice and offering; yes, they will make a vow to Yahweh and perform it.

22 And Yahweh will strike Egypt, He will strike and heal it; they will return to Yahweh, and He will be entreated by them and heal them.

23 In that day there will be a highway from Egypt to Assyria, and the Assyrian will come into Egypt and the Egyptian into Assyria, and the Egyptians will serve with the Assyrians.

24 In that day Israel will be one of three with Egypt and Assyria — a blessing in the midst of the land,

25 whom Yahweh of hosts shall bless, saying, "Blessed is Egypt My people, and Assyria the work of My hands, and Israel My inheritance."

Those Philistines (Palestinians) who remain in the land will also convert to the worship of Elohim—and they will be like the leaders of Judah and the Jerusalemites.

Zecharyah (Zechariah) 9:6-7

6 "A mixed race shall settle in Ashdod, And I will cut off the pride of the Philistines.

7 I will take away the blood from his mouth, And the abominations from between his teeth. But he who remains, even he shall be for our Elohim, And shall be like a leader in Judah, And Ekron like a Yebusite [Jerusalemite]."

We give the full details in *Revelation and the End Times*, but in the next chapter we will summarize the basics of the end times, so we can understand what we as Nazarene Israelites should do, and what we should not do, so we can be safe.

However, the most important thing we can ever do is to hear and obey His voice. No matter what is happening in the world around us, remaining in obedience to His voice is our number one priority at all times.

The End Time Sequence

Prophecy is not given to us so we can know the future. Rather, we are given prophecy so that when the events prophesied take place, they will confirm and strengthen our faith. Nonetheless, if we study the prophecies, we can learn some things—and not only can these things help us to stay out of harm's way, they can also show us how to please Yahweh.

In *Revelation and the End Times* we show how the white horse of Revelation is papal Christianity.

> Hitgalut (Revelation) 6:2
> 2 And I looked, and behold, a white horse. He who sat on it had a bow; and a crown was given to him, and he went out conquering and to conquer.

Yeshua will return on a white horse (Revelation 19:11), but this horse (above) is not Yeshua's horse, because it goes out conquering, and to conquer (i.e., dominate). The man on this horse has a crown, symbolic of temporal (governmental) authority. This speaks of how the Roman Empire used military force to spread its hybrid sun-worship faith, and how the Christian kings of Europe drew power and authority from the papacy.

When the Protestants realized that the pope was the anti-Messiah, they began to question why they should serve the pope's kings. Then when the Enlightenment took place in the late seventeenth and eighteenth centuries, not only did men turn away from Scripture, they also turned away from the pope's kings. This allowed the rise of the red horse, which represents populist rule (socialism, communism, and democracy [voting]).

Hitgalut (Revelation) 6:4
4 Another horse, fiery red, went out. And it was granted to the one who sat on it to take peace from the earth, and that people should kill one another; and there was given to him a great sword.

It isn't hard to see how communist (red) Russia and red China qualify as the red horse, but the red horse also operates in democracy. The reason democracy is also of the red horse is that Yahweh wants us to seek His face, and let Him choose our leaders for us. In contrast, in a democracy we choose our own leaders (and we ignore Yahweh's election and anointment entirely). Even if our leaders are believers, bypassing Yahweh's election and anointment means we also bypass His blessings and protection. Further, as we will see, we open ourselves up to abuse by the black horse (the Illuminist money power).

American Christians celebrate their independence from King George on July 4, but what many of them do not realize is that most of America's founding fathers were Freemasons, and they chose July 4 for occult reasons. July 4 falls 13 days after the Summer Solstice, which is their Day of Lithia. It also falls 66 days after the Festival of Beltane on April 30 (which is the highest day on the Druidic witch's calendar). All of these things have great significance in witchcraft. The Bavarian Illuminati also specifically celebrate the American Independence Day because this is when the Christians first began turning away from their protectors (the Christian white horse kings) en masse, and began embracing populist red horse democracy. This made Christians a much easier prey. In celebration, the Illuminati have put the Roman numerals MDCCLXXVI (1776) at the base of Satan's pyramid, on the back of the Unites States one-dollar bill.

Although the Christian kings derived their power from the pope (the anti-Messiah), and although they were loyal to the pope, they had every incentive to teach their subjects to believe Scripture, because the only reason they had any authority was because the people believed in Christian kingship.

Men do not like to be loyal to kings, but they will do so if they realize Yahweh desires it.

Kepha Aleph (1 Peter) 2:17
17 Honor all people. Love the brotherhood. Fear Elohim. Honor the king.

Christian Europe experienced some awful kings—yet even bad kings have incentives to make sure their people believe Scripture. They also have an incentive to keep secret societies from forming and taking control. However, when people turn away from their Christian kings, there is nothing to stop occult men of power and money from buying control, and working behind the scenes in secret societies, such as the Illuminati, the Freemasons, the Bilderberg Group, etc.

When we speak of the black horse, we are talking about the Illuminati, and also the Zionist money power (which is predominantly Jewish). One might say the Zionist Illuminati have hearts as black as coal, because they seek to control the whole world by controlling all national currencies, destabilizing governments, and destroying Yeshua's worship and values. They also encourage war all over the world, which makes them even richer, because they finance all sides of these wars. In the black horse's sick and twisted world, only power, money, and control ultimately matter.

Hitgalut (Revelation) 6:5-6
5 When He opened the third seal, I heard the third living creature say, "Come and see." So I looked, and behold, a black horse, and he who sat on it had a pair of scales in his hand.
6 And I heard a voice in the midst of the four living creatures saying, "A quart of wheat for a denarius, and three quarts of barley for a denarius; and do not harm the oil and the wine."

With control of the world's money supply, the Illuminati control the Freemasons (who in turn control most governments). With control of the governments, they also control the courts and the schools. They also own most mainline media outlets, including Hollywood. The black horse's control of the world's money supply also gives it a unique ability to control the other horses. All of this leaves the black horse in a unique position to influence what the average man thinks. This control is then applied toward their ultimate goal, which is to establish a one world government with a false one world religion. As we show in *Revelation and the End Times*, their plans include relocating the pope's throne to the temple mount, and establishing a one world religion in conjunction with the Muslims and the rabbis. Many of the agreements are already signed.

The green horse is Islam. Green is Islam's primary color, and the color green can be found in almost all Islamic flags, banners, armbands, and headbands.

Hitgalut (Revelation) 6:7-8

7 When He opened the fourth seal, I heard the voice of the fourth living creature saying, "Come and see."

8 So I looked, and behold, a pale [green] horse. And the name of him who sat on it was Death, and Hades followed with him. And power was given to them over a fourth of the earth, to kill with sword, with hunger, with death, and by the beasts of the earth.

The King James Version and other mainline versions render the fourth horse as a "pale" horse, but as we explain in *Revelation and the End Times*, the Greek word here is *chloros*. Chloros means *green* (just as chlorophyll is green). Interestingly, the four tribulation colors (white, red, black, and green) show up in almost all Islamic flags. For example, below are the flags of Jordan, Afghanistan, and Kuwait.

It is also interesting that the four horses are the three Avrahamic religions, plus populism (democracy, socialism, etc.). These are the four main spiritual forces shaping our world.

White	Papal Christianity (Ephraim is lost here)
Red	Populism (Communism, democracy)
Black	Zionist Judaism (Judah is lost here)
Green	Islam (Cousin Ishmael is lost here)

Satan is the author of confusion, and the four horses certainly create confusion in that while all four horses war against each other, they are also secretly working together, in collusion. One example is how the white horse (Christianity) and the green horse (Islam) are both manifestations of the same Babylonian beast.

In *Revelation and the End Times*, we show how King Nebuchadnezzar dreamed of a statue that was set up on the earth. Its head was made of fine gold (symbolic of Babylon), its chest and arms were made of silver (Medea-Persia), its belly and thighs were of bronze (Greece), its legs were made of iron (Rome), and its feet were made of iron (Rome) mixed with clay (Islam). This symbolized a series of five successive empires which would all be Babylonian in nature. That is to say, power and authority would not be used to take care of the people and to establish Yahweh's kingdom here on earth. Rather, in Babylonian governments, power and authority are used to enslave the masses for the benefit of the elites, and to destroy Yahweh's people, and His worship.

Daniel 2:37-43
37 "You, O king [Nebuchadnezzar], are a king of kings. For the Elohim of heaven has given you a kingdom, power, strength, and glory;
38 and wherever the children of men dwell, or the beasts of the field and the birds of the heaven, He

has given them into your hand, and has made you ruler over them all — you are this head of gold.

39 But after you shall arise another kingdom inferior to yours [Medea-Persia]; then another, a third kingdom of bronze [Greece], which shall rule over all the earth [in context, the Middle East].

40 And the fourth kingdom [Rome] shall be as strong as iron, inasmuch as iron breaks in pieces and shatters everything; and like iron that crushes, that kingdom will break in pieces and crush all the others.

41 Whereas you saw the feet and toes, partly of potter's clay and partly of iron, the kingdom shall be divided; yet the strength of the iron shall be in it, just as you saw the iron [Rome] mixed with ceramic clay [Islam].

42 And as the toes of the feet were partly of iron and partly of clay, so the kingdom [New World Order] shall be partly strong and partly fragile.

43 As you saw iron mixed with ceramic clay, they will mingle with the seed of men; but they will not adhere to one another, just as iron [Rome] does not mix with clay [Islam]."

In *Revelation and the End Times* we show how the iron represents Rome, and the clay represents Islam. We also show how Islam grew out of the Roman Empire. The succession of empires is shown in the table below.

Body part:	Earthly empire:
1. Head of gold	Babylon (Iraq)
2. Chest and arms of silver	Medea-Persia (Iran)
3. Belly and thighs of bronze	Macedonia (Greece)
4. Two legs of iron (west/east)	Roman Empire (W/E)
5. Two feet of iron and clay	Christianity and Islam

In *Revelation and the End Times* we show how the administration of the Roman Empire was split into two parts (in 293 CE), thus forming the western and eastern "legs" of the Roman Empire (corresponding to the two iron legs on the statue).

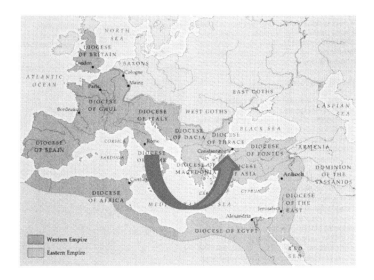

In 330 CE, Emperor Constantine moved his capital from Rome to Byzantium (in the eastern leg), renaming it Constantinople. Later, the eastern leg of the Roman Empire became the Byzantine Empire. The Byzantine Empire was later conquered by the Muslims, and it became the Ottoman Empire. Constantinople was then renamed Istanbul (Turkey).

While Christians and Muslims have fought many wars, both have also secretly colluded behind the scenes to destroy their mutual enemy, Judah. Both Christianity and Islam are secretly manifestations of the same Babylonian Empire, much like the Democrats and the Republicans seem to fight against each other, but both secretly take part of the red horse democratic system.

Occult documents reveal that the ultimate plan is to engineer a nuclear war in the Middle East between Islam and Brother Judah. This will be used to sell the world on the alleged need for a New World Order (i.e., toes of iron mixed with clay, Daniel 2:43). The NWO will supposedly save mankind from destruction.

Albert Pike was a 33rd degree Freemason, and the leader of Freemasonry in North America. In 1871, he wrote a letter to a fellow Freemason named Mazzini, in which he outlined an occult vision he received concerning three world wars that would culminate in a Satanic one world order. The following are extracts of his letter to Mazzini, showing how three world wars have been planned for many generations.

> "The First World War must be brought about in order to permit the Illuminati [black horse] to overthrow the power of the Czars in Russia and of making that country a fortress of atheistic Communism [red horse]. The divergences caused by the "agentur" [agents] of the Illuminati between the British and Germanic Empires will be used to foment this war. At the end of the war, Communism will be built and used in order to destroy the other governments and in order to weaken the religions." [Commander William Guy Carr, *Satan: Prince of This World*]

World War 1 was fomented principally by alliances surrounding England on one side, and Germany on the other. The German leader, Otto von Bismarck, was a co-conspirator of Albert Pike.

> "The Second World War must be fomented by taking advantage of the differences between the Fascists and the political Zionists [black horse].

This war must be brought about so that Nazism is destroyed and that the political Zionism [black horse] be strong enough to institute a sovereign state of Israel in Palestine. During the Second World War, International Communism [red horse] must become strong enough in order to balance Christendom [white horse], which would be then restrained and held in check until the time when we would need it for the final social cataclysm." [Commander William Guy Carr, *Satan: Prince of This World*]

As predicted, a sovereign Zionist state of Israel was created in Palestine after World War 2, and the communist red horse forces balanced out the white horse Christian west. We should also note that the terms Nazism and Zionism were not known in 1871, when this letter was written, but that the Illuminati invented both these movements.

"The Third World War must be fomented by taking advantage of the differences caused by the "agentur" of the "Illuminati" between the political Zionists and the leaders of Islamic World. The war must be conducted in such a way that Islam [the Muslim World] and political Zionism [the State of Israel] mutually destroy each other. Meanwhile the other nations, once more divided on this issue will be constrained to fight to the point of complete physical, moral, spiritual and economical exhaustion....We shall unleash the Nihilists and the atheists, and we shall provoke a formidable social cataclysm which in all its horror will show clearly to the nations the effect of absolute atheism, origin of savagery and of the most bloody turmoil. Then everywhere, the citizens, obliged to defend themselves against the world minority of revolutionaries, will exterminate those destroyers of civilization, and the multitude, disillusioned with Christianity, whose deistic spirits will from that moment be without compass or direction, anxious for an ideal, but without knowing where to render its adoration, will receive the true light through the universal manifestation of the pure doctrine of Lucifer, brought finally out in the public view. This manifestation will result from the general reactionary movement which will follow the destruction of Christianity and atheism, both conquered and exterminated at the same time." [Commander William Guy Carr, *Satan: Prince of This World*]

We could easily dismiss Albert Pike's letter if it did not line up so well with Scripture. It does seem that a nuclear conflict between the Islamic world and Israel could be a reality in the relatively near future. For example, what would happen if Iran were to get the bomb, and declare a nuclear war on Israel?

What if the United Nations asks the pope to step in and broker a peace deal with the Muslims, which he can do because of his longstanding ties with Islam?

What if the UN were then to ask the pope to move his throne to the temple mount, and establish a temple there, with the outer courtyard open to all the religions of the world? And what if other Illuminist government leaders hailed the pope as a hero, for establishing a "peace that is no peace"?

Would such a scenario fulfill 2 Thessalonians 2:3-4, which speaks of a man of sin (a man of torahlessness) sitting in a temple of Elohim, showing himself as Elohim (Vicarius Philii Dei)?

> Thessaloniqim Bet (2 Thessalonians) 2:3-4
> 3 Let no one deceive you by any means; for that Day will not come unless the falling away comes first, and the man of sin is revealed, the son of perdition,
> 4 who opposes and exalts himself above all that is called Elohim or that is worshiped, so that he sits as Elohim in the temple of Elohim, showing himself that he is Elohim.

In *Revelation and the End Times* we show how the Vatican and the Dome of the Rock are all temples of Jupiter (Satan). Note the domed cupola, with the nipple on top, common to each temple.

We cover the timeline in detail in *Revelation and the End Times*, but here is a simplified version.

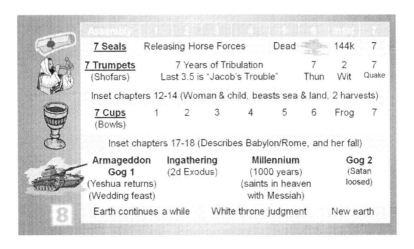

Assembly	1	2	3		4		5	inset	7
7 Seals	Releasing Horse Forces				Dead			144k	7
7 Trumpets (Shofars)	7 Years of Tribulation Last 3.5 is "Jacob's Trouble"						7 Thun	2 Wit	7 Quake
Inset chapters 12-14 (Woman & child, beasts sea & land, 2 harvests)									
7 Cups (Bowls)	1	2	3	4	5	6		Frog	7
Inset chapters 17-18 (Describes Babylon/Rome, and her fall)									
Armageddon Gog 1 (Yeshua returns) (Wedding feast)	**Ingathering** (2d Exodus)			**Millennium** (1000 years) (saints in heaven with Messiah)				**Gog 2** (Satan loosed)	
Earth continues a while		White throne judgment						New earth	

To understand the timeline, think of how a woman gestates and gives birth. The seals (horse forces) play out over hundreds of years, like how she carries her child for many months. The trumpets (tribulation) are like her contractions, and the seven thunders are like her cries when the pain grips her. The cups pouring out are like her water breaking. At the end of the cups, a "man child" will be born, who will be redeemed Israel.

There are other analogies, but at trumpet 7, the entire Babylonian system will fall. People talk about fleeing this or that country, but that misses the point. Babylon is a spirit, and when it falls, Babylonian Christianity, and hence Islam (and also rabbinic Judaism) will come crashing down, along with all red horse governments.

258

This will look like complete and total societal collapse. In the aftermath of this collapse, the Elohim of heaven will set up a kingdom of His saints, which shall never be destroyed, and the kingdom shall not be left to other people. It shall break in pieces and destroy all of the other kingdoms (Christianity, Populism, Judaism, and Islam), and it shall stand until the earth is destroyed.

> Daniel 2:44
> 44 "And in the days of these kings the Elohim of heaven will set up a kingdom which shall never be destroyed; and the kingdom shall not be left to other people; it shall break in pieces and consume all these kingdoms, and it shall stand forever."

Prophecy is not given to us so we can know the future. Rather, we are given prophecy so that when the events prophesied take place, they will confirm and strengthen our faith. Nonetheless, if we study the prophecies we can learn some things—and not only can these things help us to stay out of harm's way, they can also show us how to please Yahweh, no matter what the future holds.

If you want to increase your chances of surviving the tribulation, then the next chapter is for you.

Becoming Yeshua's Helpmeet

We have covered a lot of ground in this book, but in this closing chapter, let us put things in perspective—because without this perspective, we will not be able to please our Husband.

Yahweh created the woman as a helper for the man.

> B'reisheet (Genesis) 2:18
> 18 And Yahweh Elohim said, "It is not good that man should be alone; I will make him a helper comparable [corresponding] to him."

While Havvah (Eve) was a real woman, she also represents Israel, who is in training to become Yeshua's bride. But if Israel is supposed to be Yeshua's bride, and a bride is a helper, then aren't we supposed to be helping Yeshua?

But how can we help Yeshua? In earlier chapters we saw that Yeshua was sent as Messiah the Prince (נגיד), who is the commander of the armies of Elohim.

> Daniel 9:25
> 25 "Know therefore and understand, that from the going forth of the command to restore and build Jerusalem until Messiah the Prince (נגיד), there shall be seven weeks and sixty-two weeks. The street shall be built again, and the wall, even in troublesome times."

Yeshua's mission was to proclaim release to the spiritual captives, and to set at liberty those who were spiritually oppressed (by the rabbis).

Luqa (Luke) 4:18-19
18 "The Spirit of Yahweh is upon Me, because He has anointed Me to preach the Good News to the poor. He has sent Me to heal the brokenhearted, to proclaim liberty to the captives and recovery of sight to the blind, to set at liberty those who are oppressed, and
19 "to proclaim the acceptable year of Yahweh...."

The problem is that, as we saw earlier, a *nagiyd* (נגיד) is defined as a commander who leads from the front. Yet Yeshua is not here, so the only way He can lead from the front is to lead through His body, Israel. That is why He gave His body (i.e., His bride, Israel) the job of fulfilling the Great Commission until He returns.

Mattityahu (Matthew) 28:18-20
18 And Yeshua came and spoke to them, saying, "All authority has been given to Me in heaven and on earth.
19 Go therefore and make disciples of all the nations, immersing them in the name of the Father and of the Son and of the Set apart Spirit,
20 teaching them to observe all things that I have commanded you; and behold, I am with you always, even to the end of the age." Amein.

Yeshua tells us plainly that when He does come, He will reward every man according to his work.

Hitgalut (Revelation) 22:12
12 "And behold, I am coming quickly, and My reward is with Me, to give to every one according to his work."

In other words, Yeshua wants a bride whose heart is set to help Him build His kingdom. He wants a bride who has proven that she loves Him enough to sacrifice her life in the world for Him, just as He gave His life in the world for her.

Friend, are we sacrificing our lives in the world for Him, just as He gave His life in the world for us?

Really?

Yeshua asked us to build Him a kingdom while He is away. Those are Yeshua's instructions. It is Yeshua's torah. So then, friend, the only question is, are we seeking to obey Yeshua's torah out of an eager love, and a burning desire to please Him? Or are we just pretending?

So many people seem to believe they are "keeping" Yeshua's torah because they read from the Levitical torah. They assume they are "disciples," even though they neither join the priesthood, nor support it. They do not seek to be Yeshua's helpers. They seek simply to rest on His rest days, eat His spiritual food, and talk.

Friend, if you were Yeshua, and you could have any woman you wanted, who would you want? Would you want to marry an interested onlooker? Or would you want to marry a bride who has proven the depths of her devotion to you, and her willingness to sacrifice and endure hardships for you and your great name?

Let us ask ourselves what kind of bride Yeshua would want—and then let us seek to become that kind of bride for Him, so we can love and serve Him with all of our heart, all of our soul, and with all of our strength.

Devarim (Deuteronomy) 6:5
5 You shall love Yahweh your Elohim with all your
heart, with all your soul, and with all your strength.

Mattityahu (Matthew) 22:36-40
36 "Teacher, which is
the great commandment in the Torah?"
37 Yeshua said to him, "'You shall love Yahweh your
Elohim with all your heart, with all your soul,
and with all your mind.'
38 This is the first and great commandment.
39 And the second is like it:
'You shall love your neighbor as yourself.'
40 On these two commandments hang
all the Torah and the Prophets."

Are we really doing it?

Support Our Work:

Nazarene Israel is reestablishing the original Nazarene faith in the modern day.

Yahweh promises to bless those who cheerfully give to His work (e.g., Exodus 25:2, Malachi 3:10). Yahweh does not lie.

If Yahweh leads you to send a voluntary offering to His work, you can send it electronically through the website at www.nazareneisrael.org or through the post to:

Nazarene Israel
P.O. Box 2905
Denton, TX 76202
USA

All monies are carefully and prayerfully used to fulfill the Great Commission, and to restore the original first century faith to the land of Israel.

May Yahweh multiply blessings to you.

Amein.

Made in the USA
Charleston, SC
28 July 2014